This Book Belongs To:

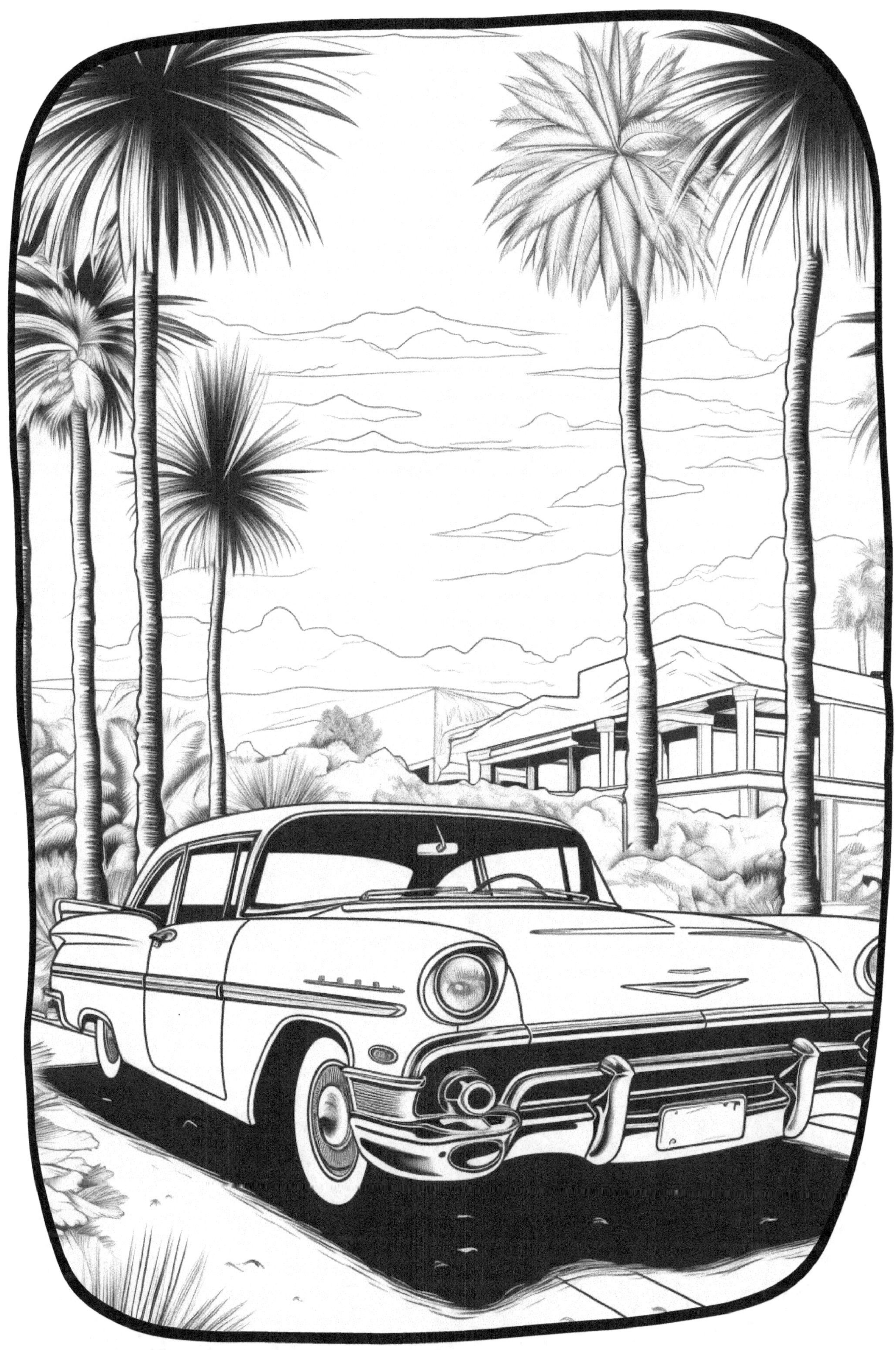

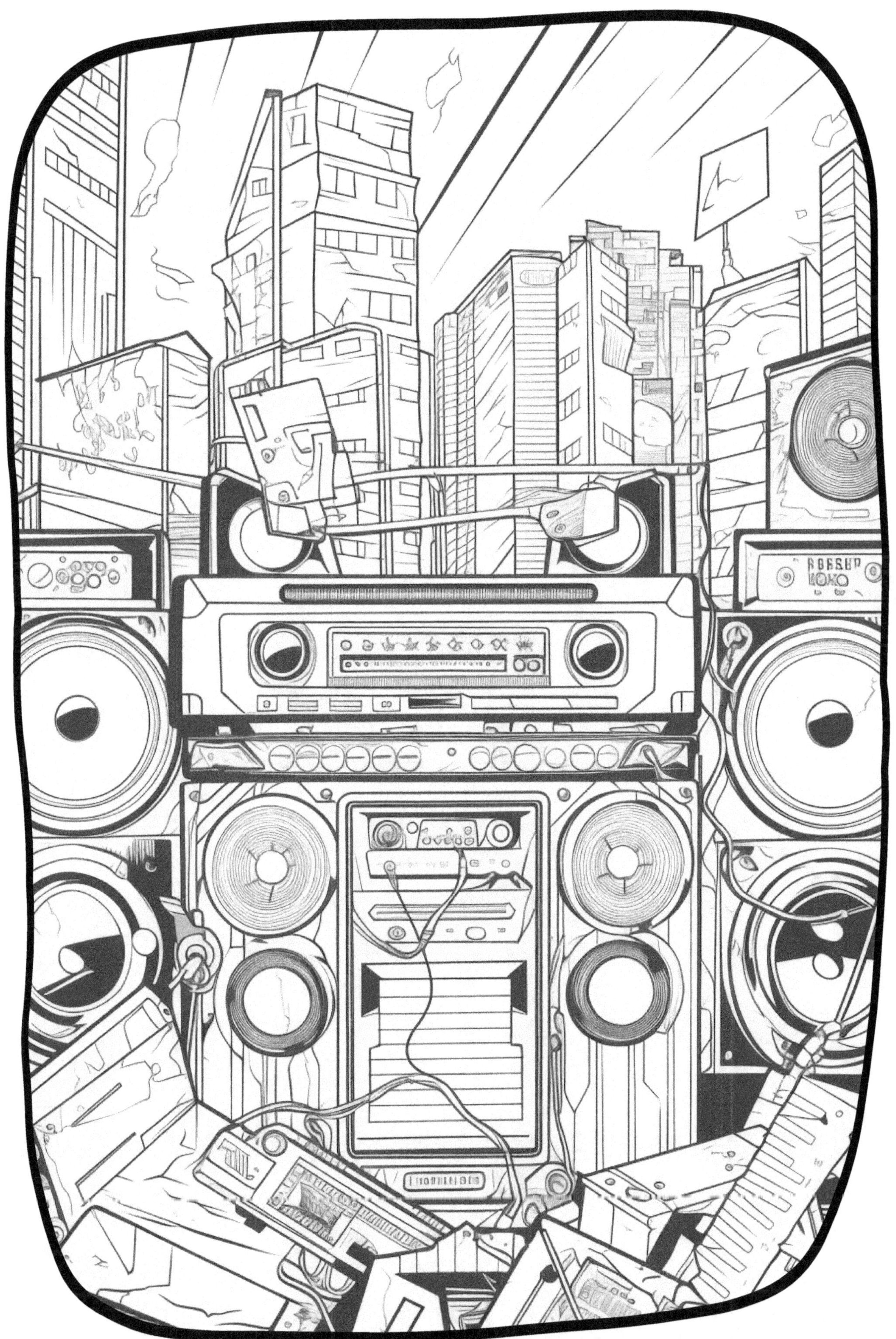

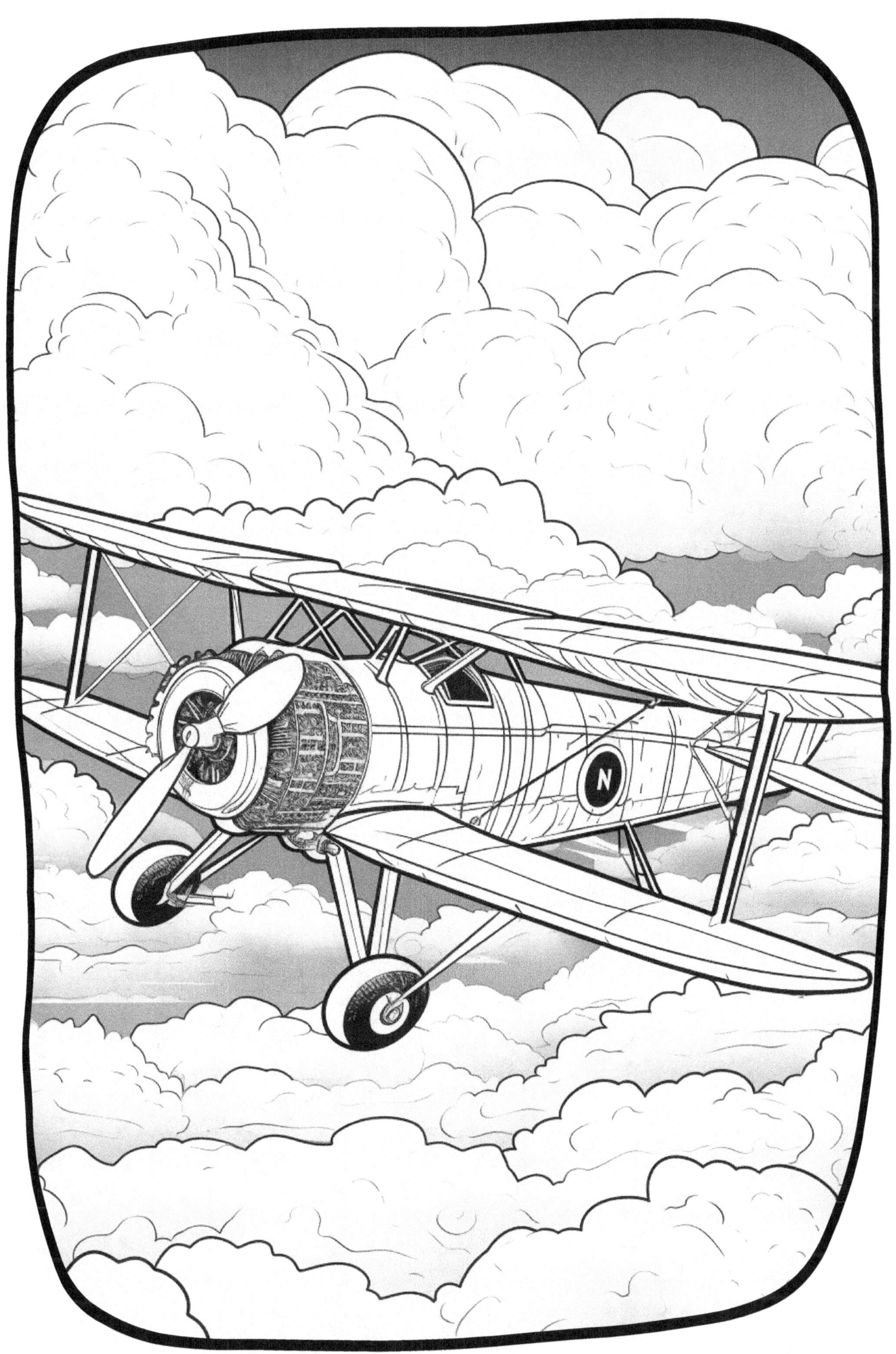

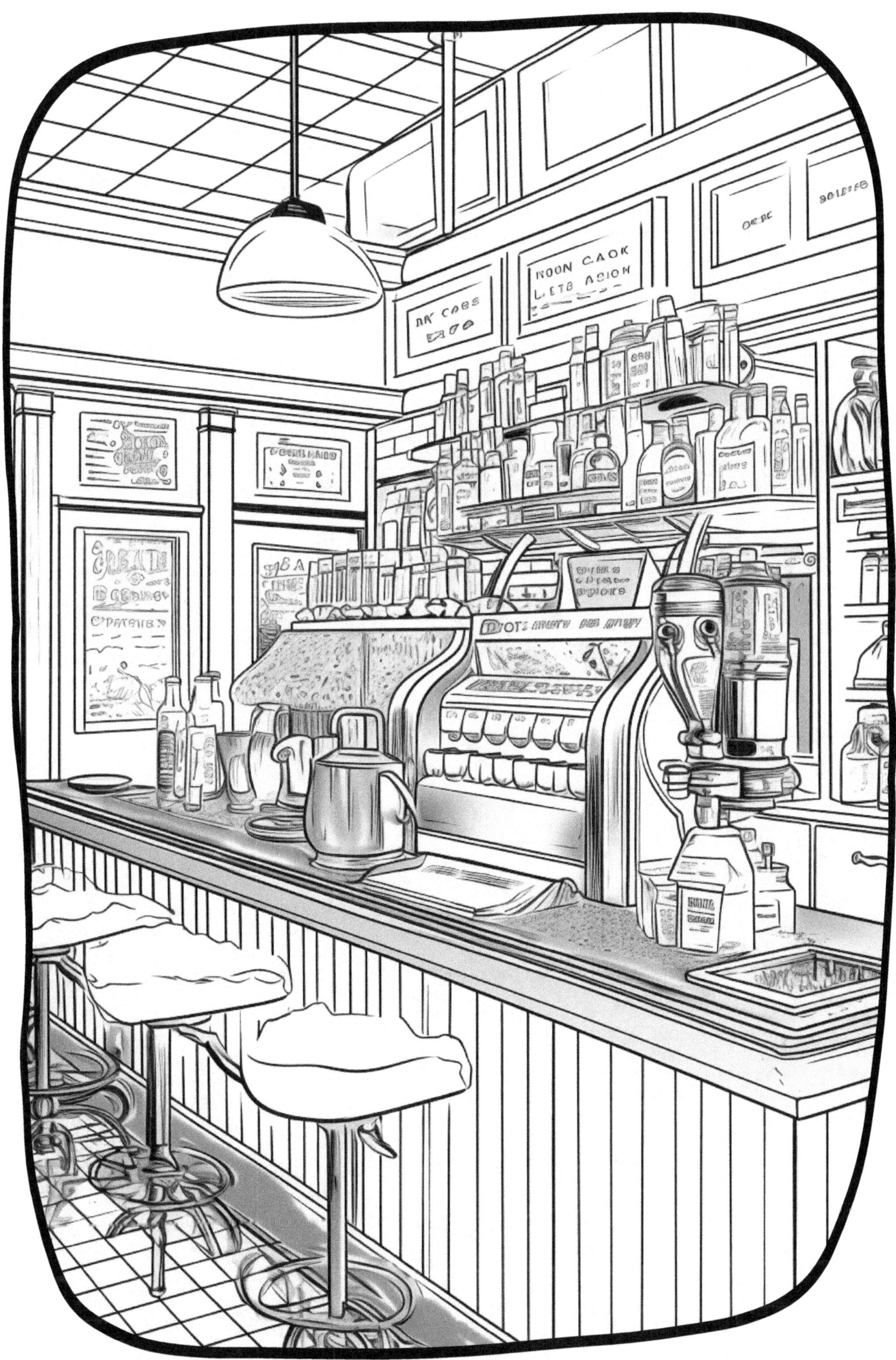

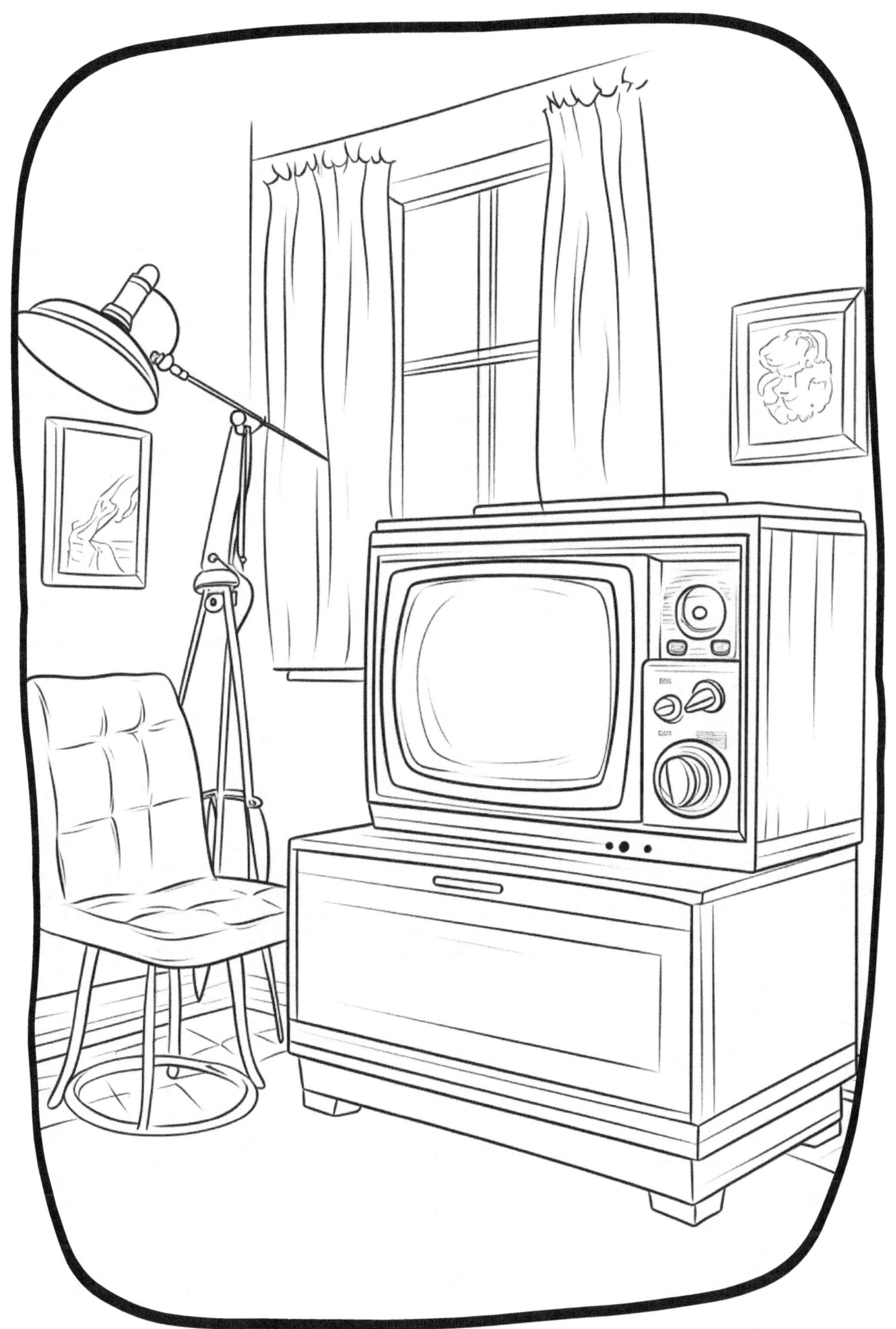

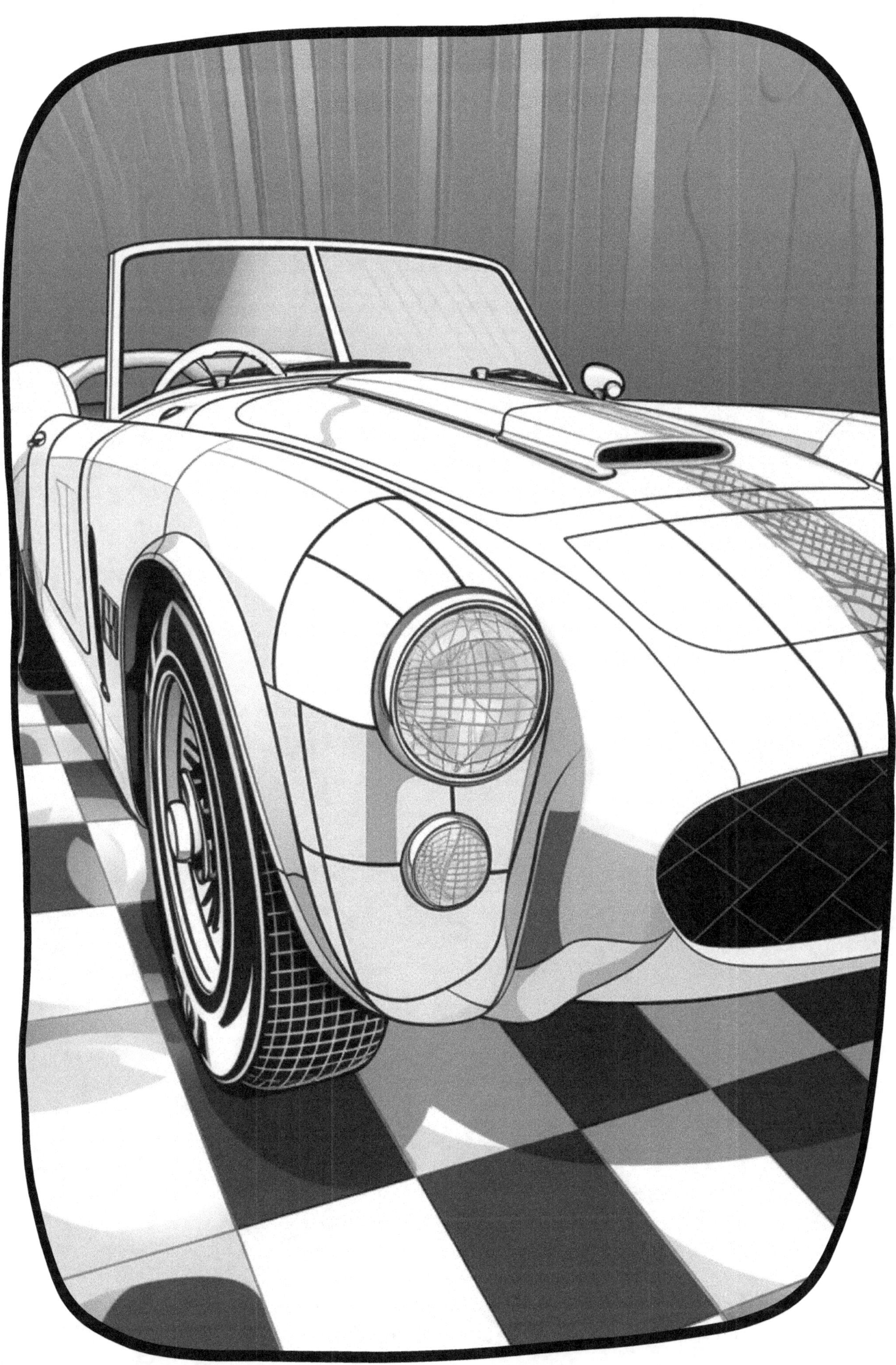

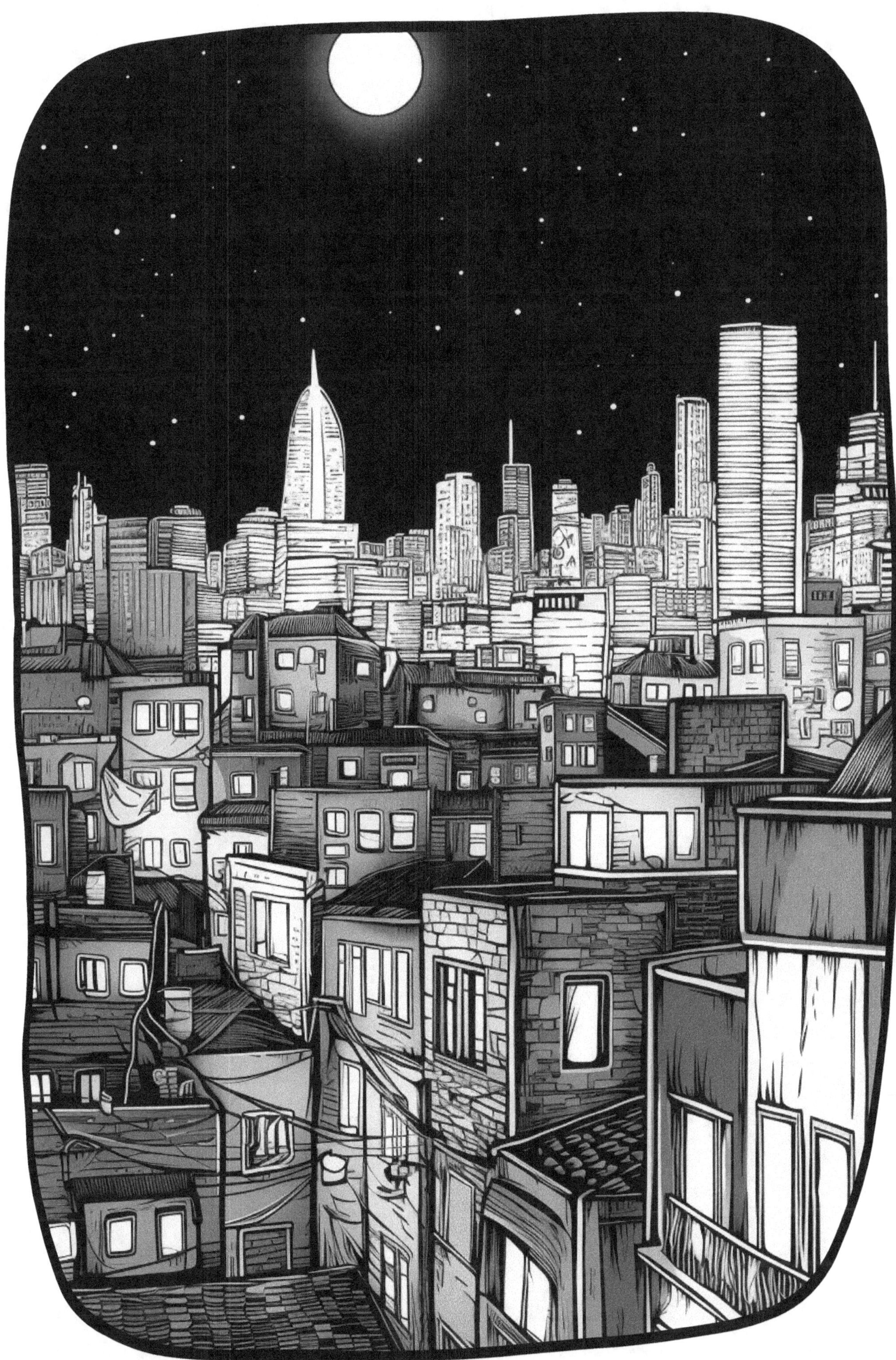

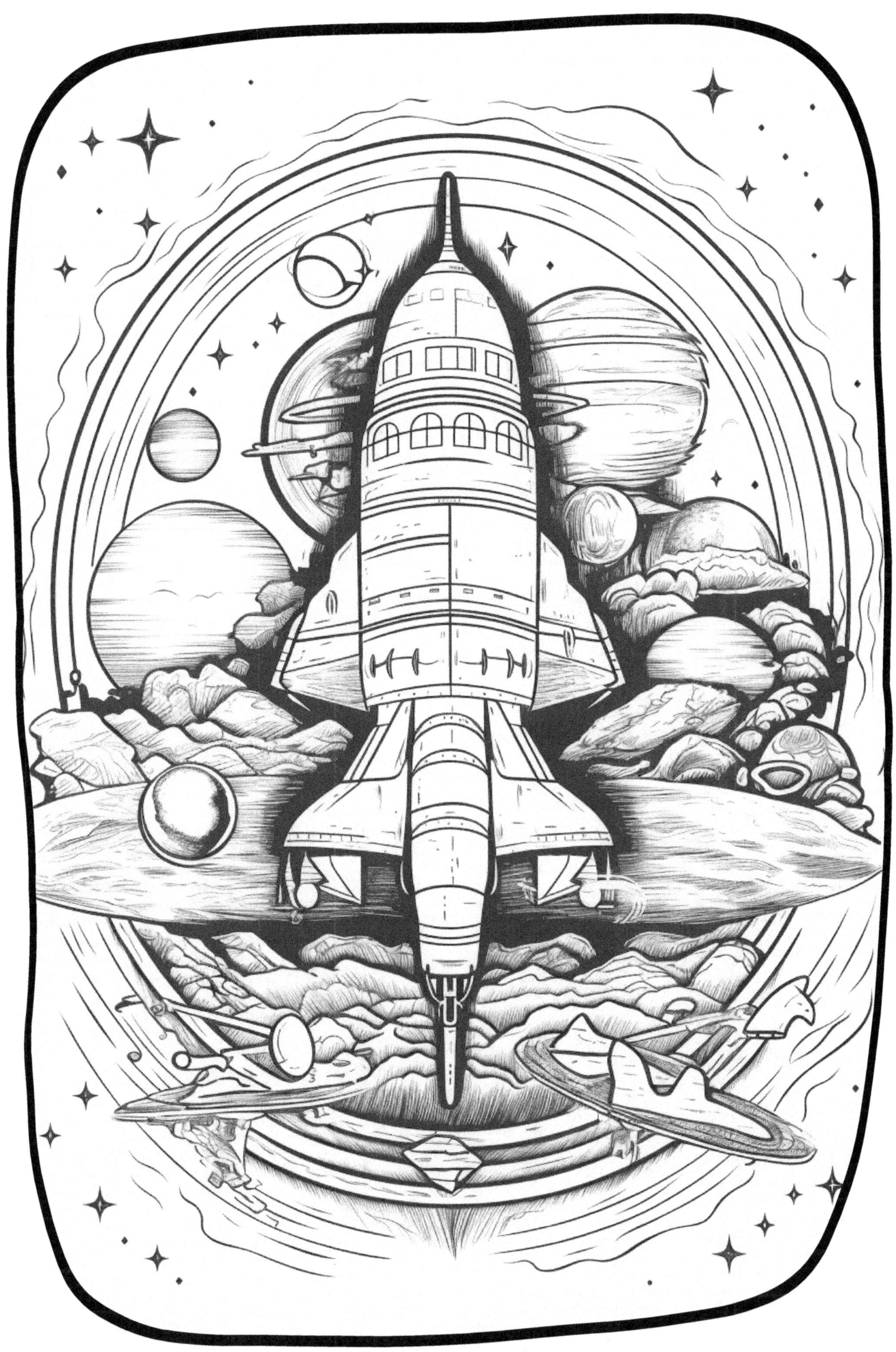

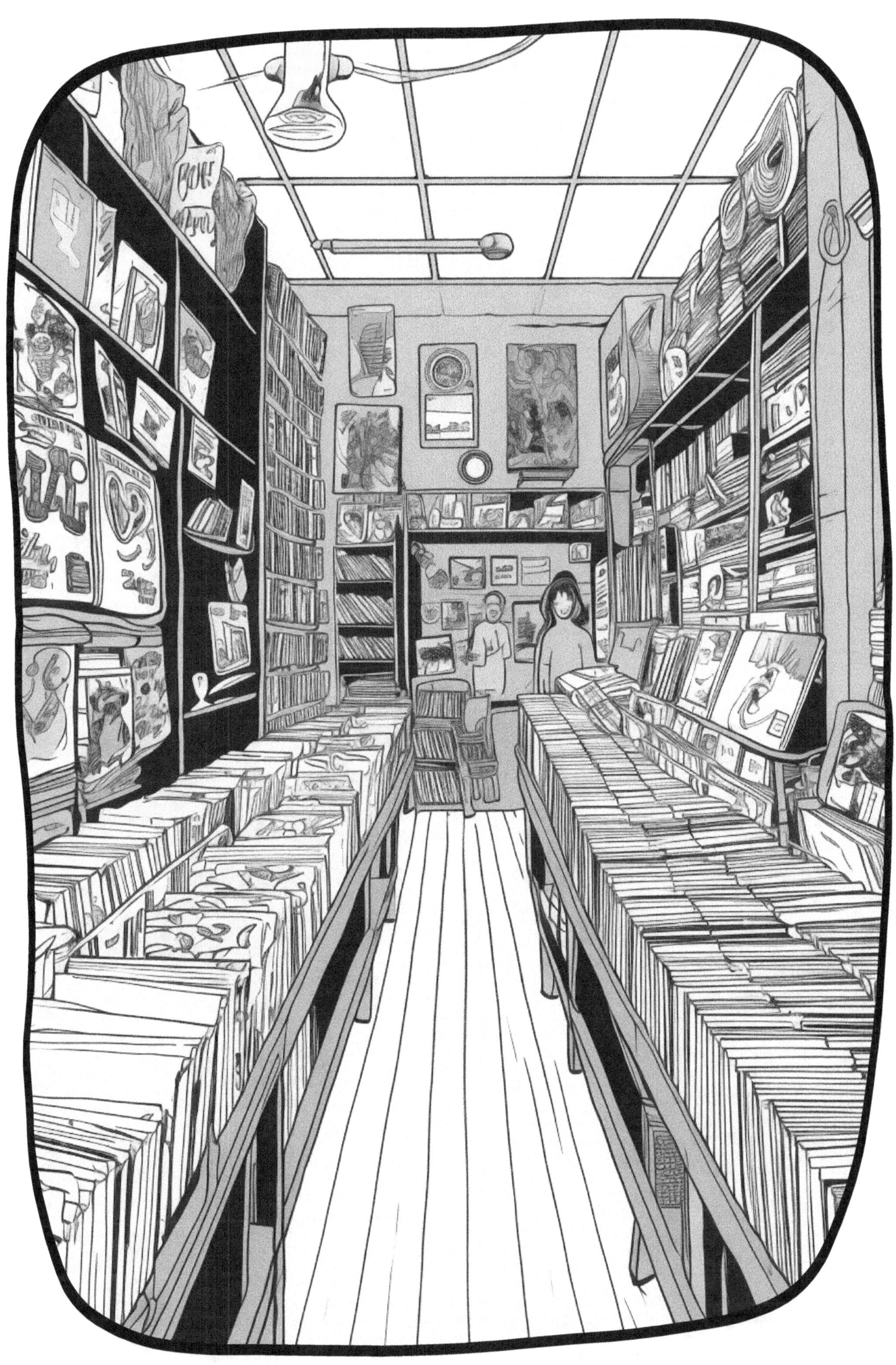

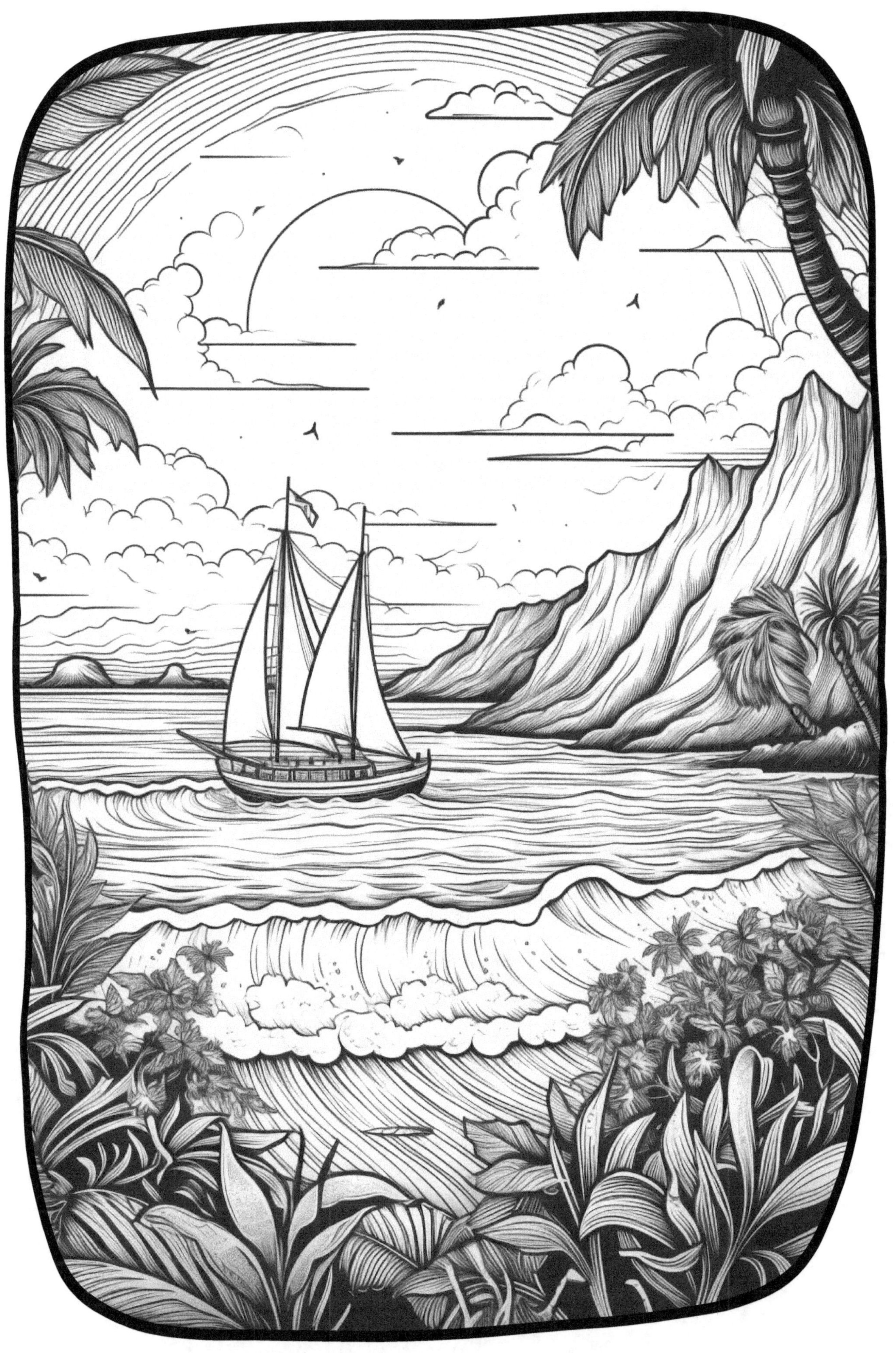

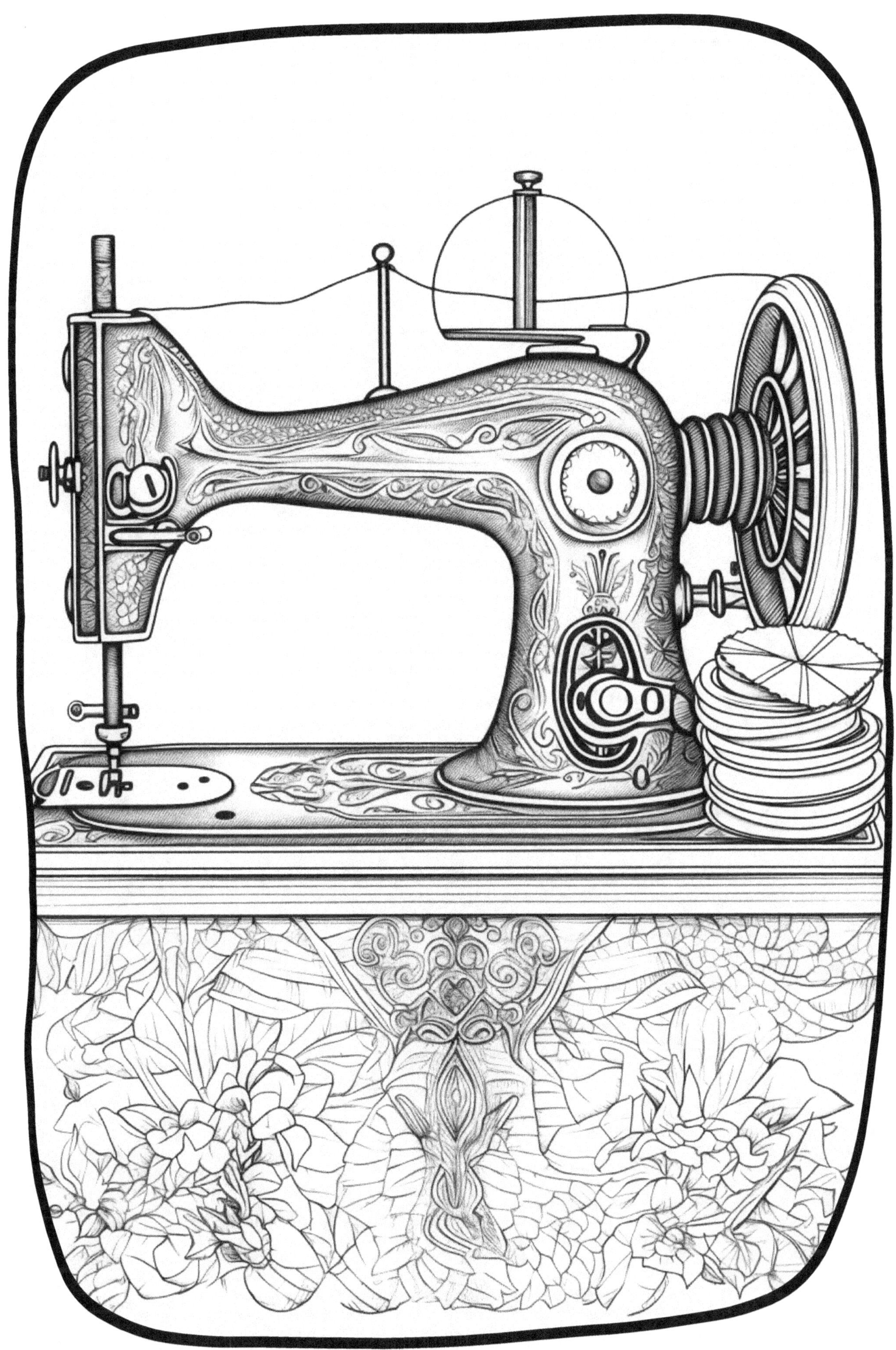

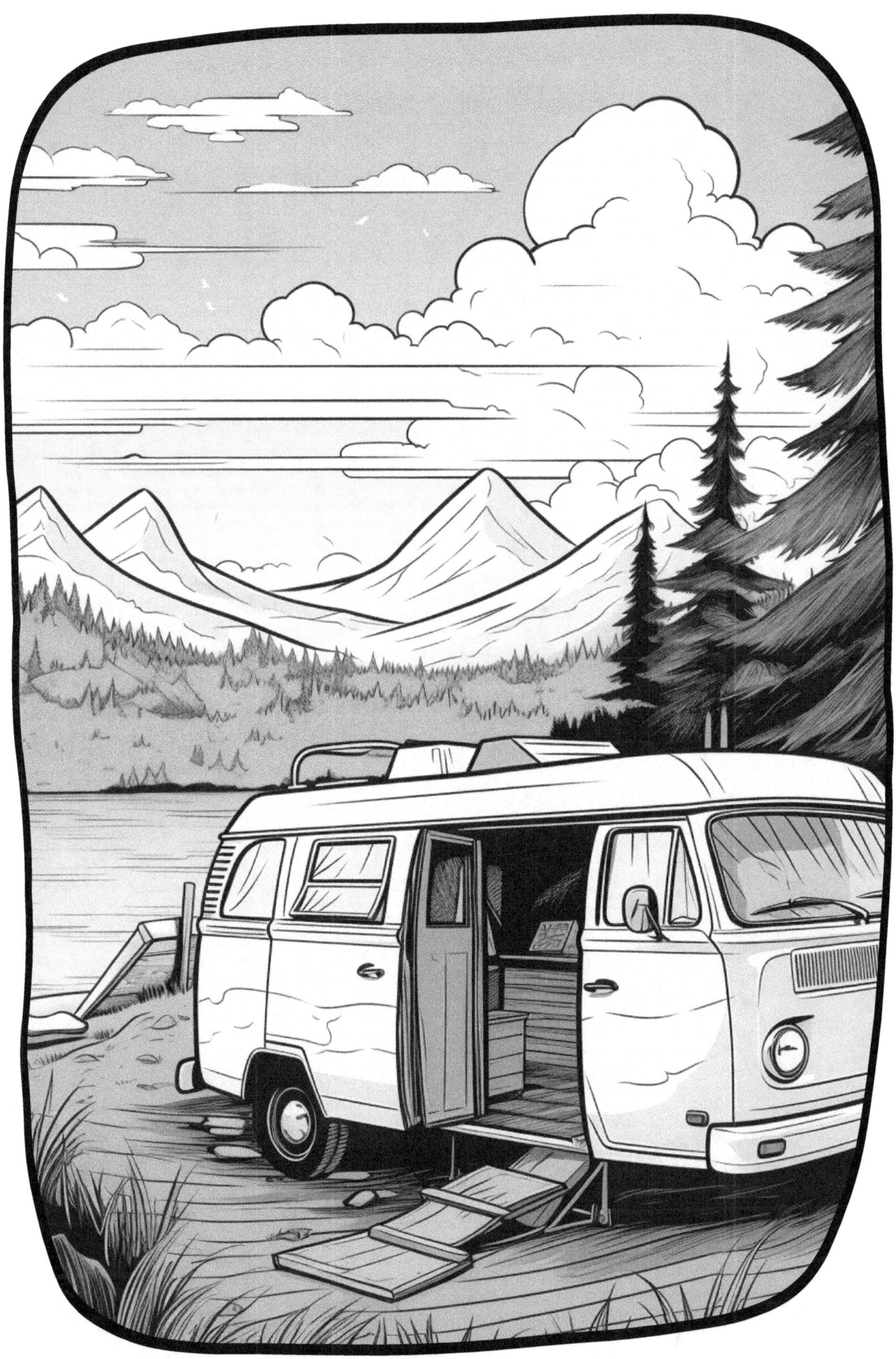

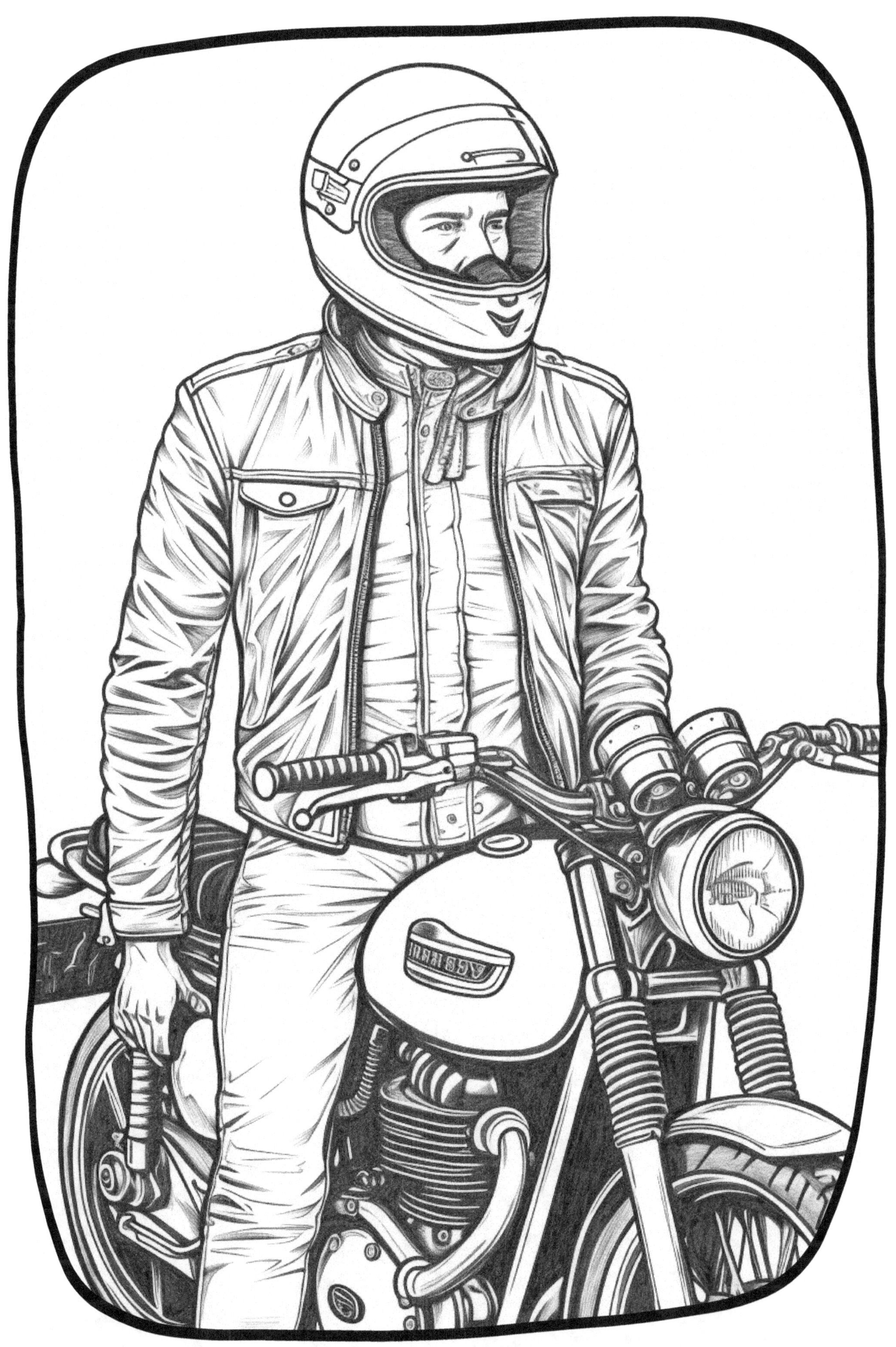

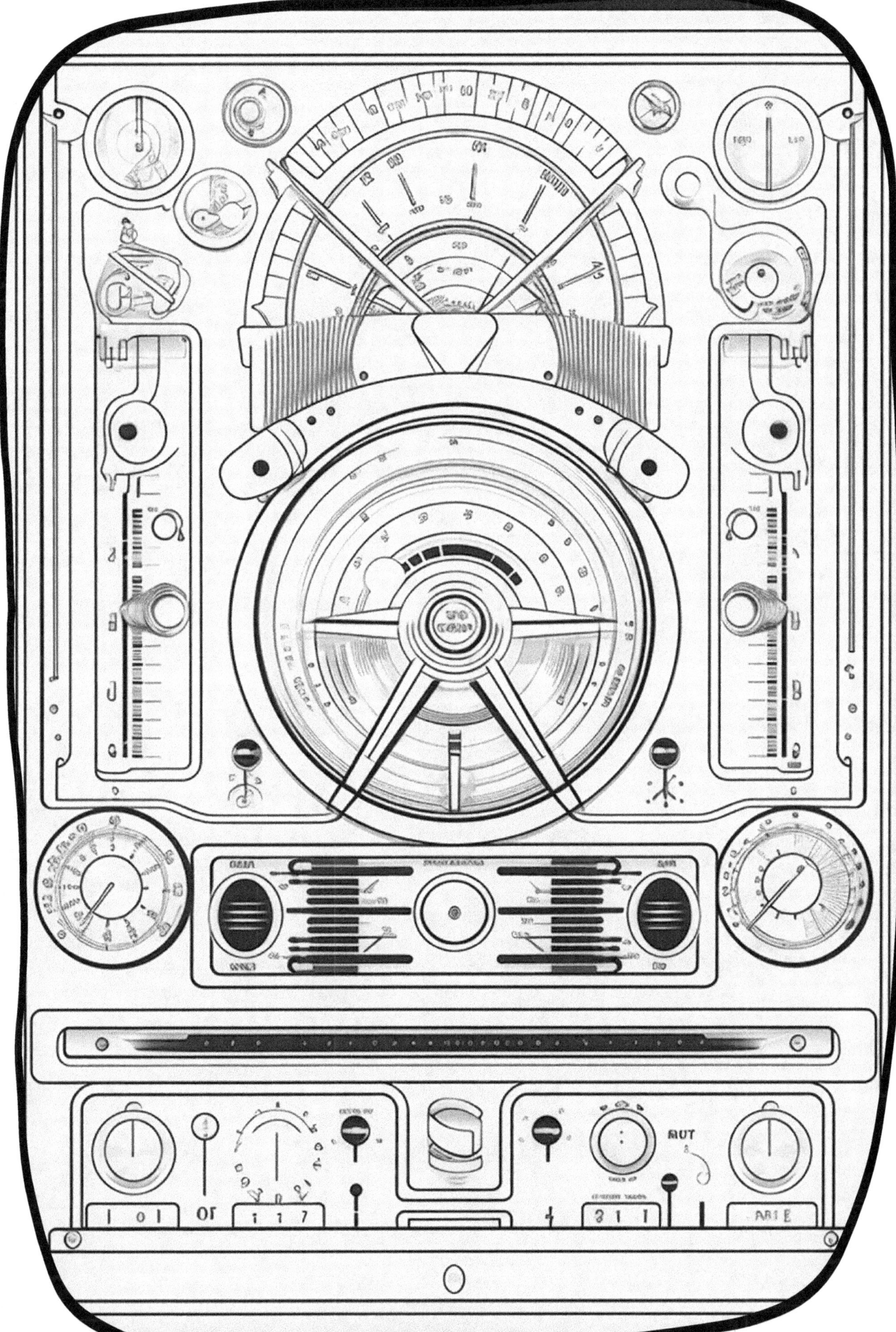

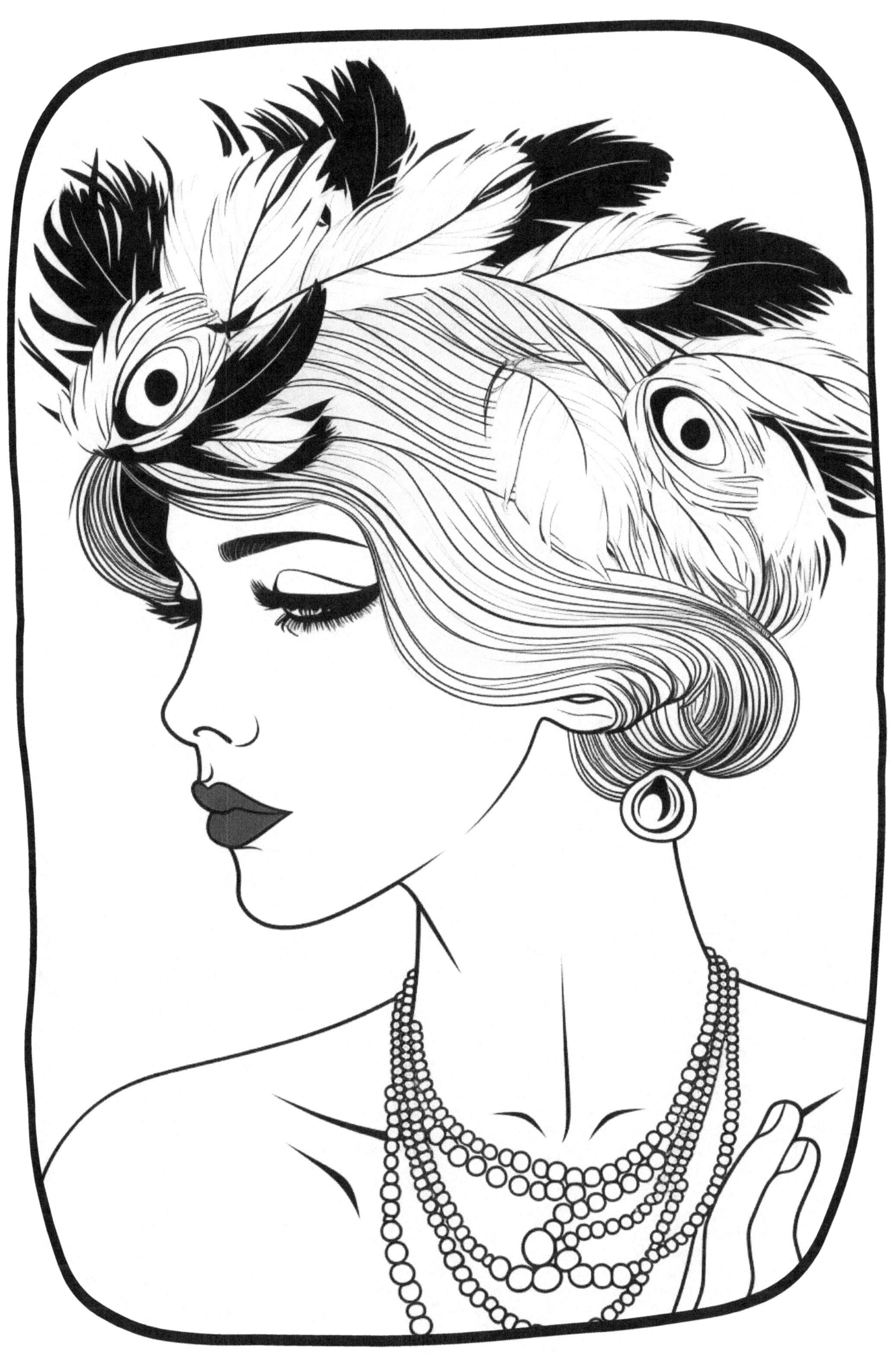

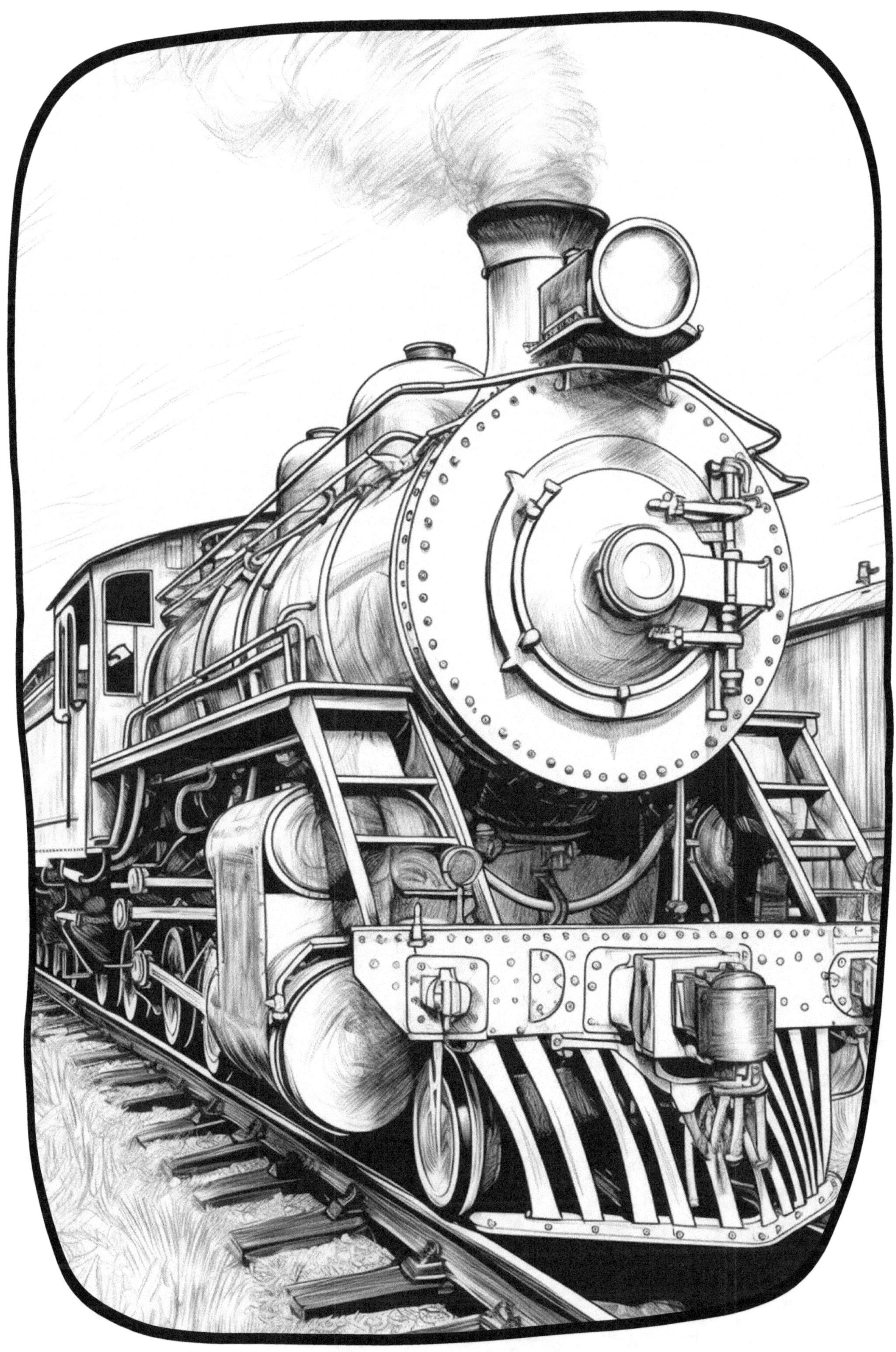

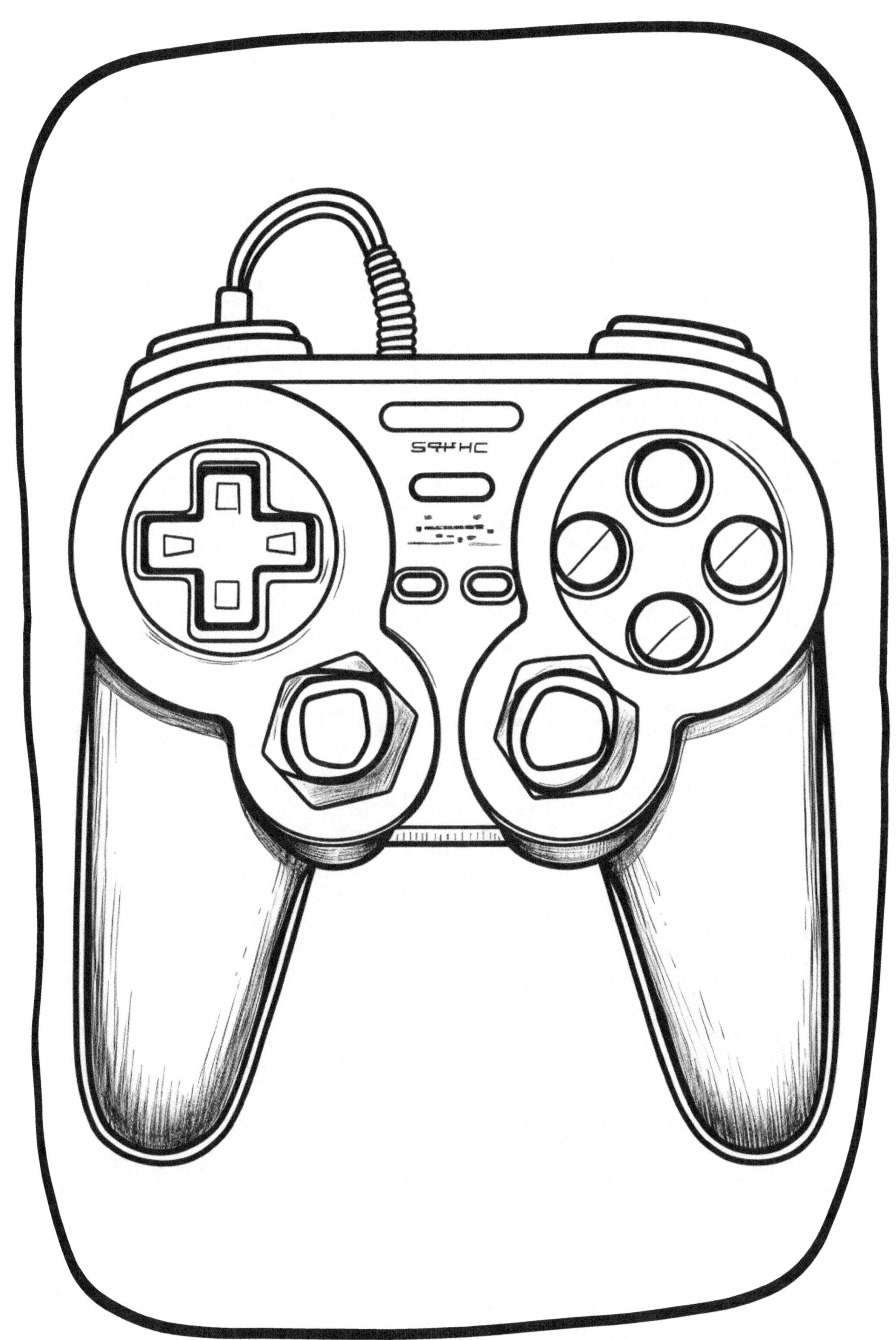

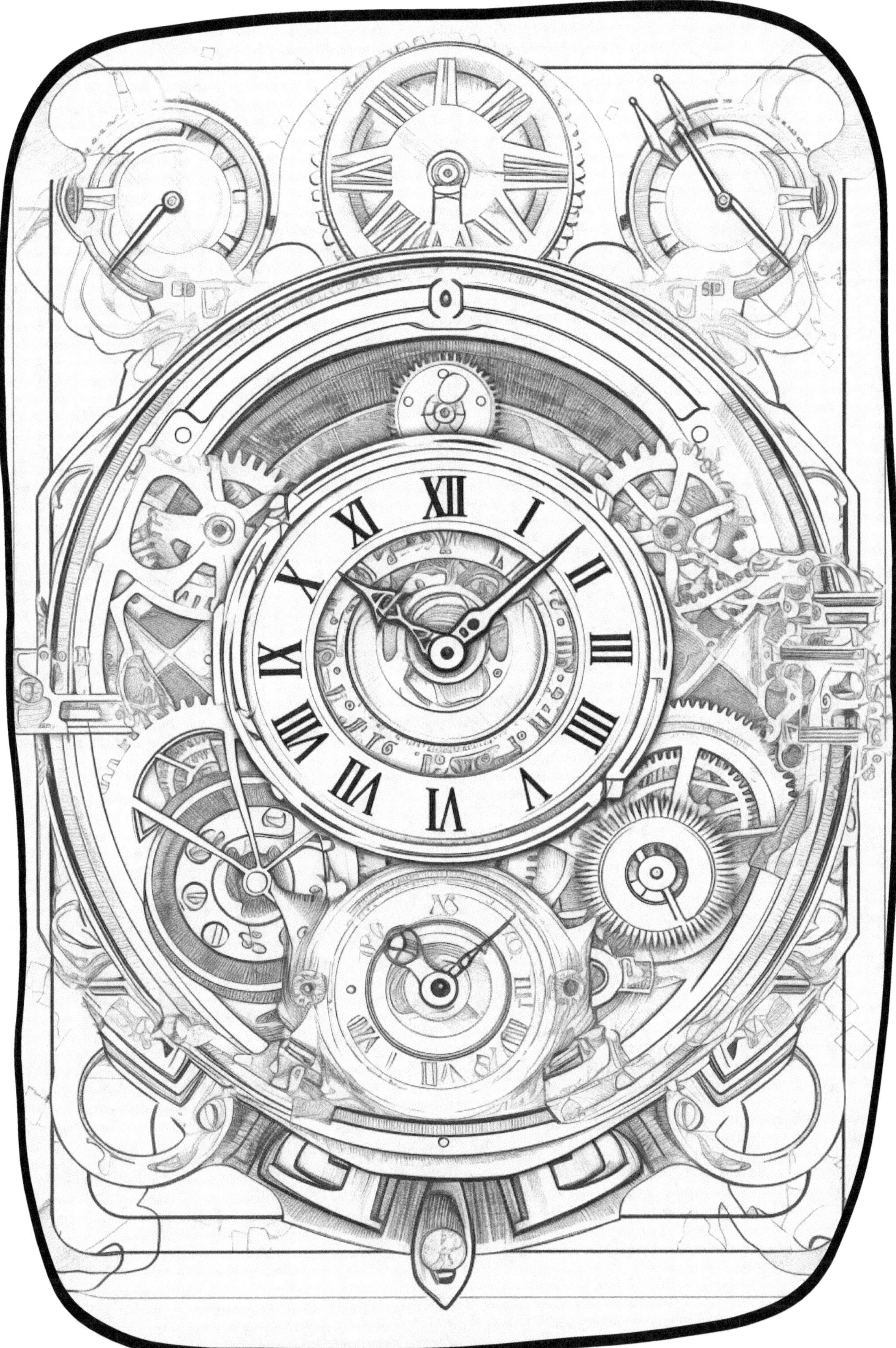

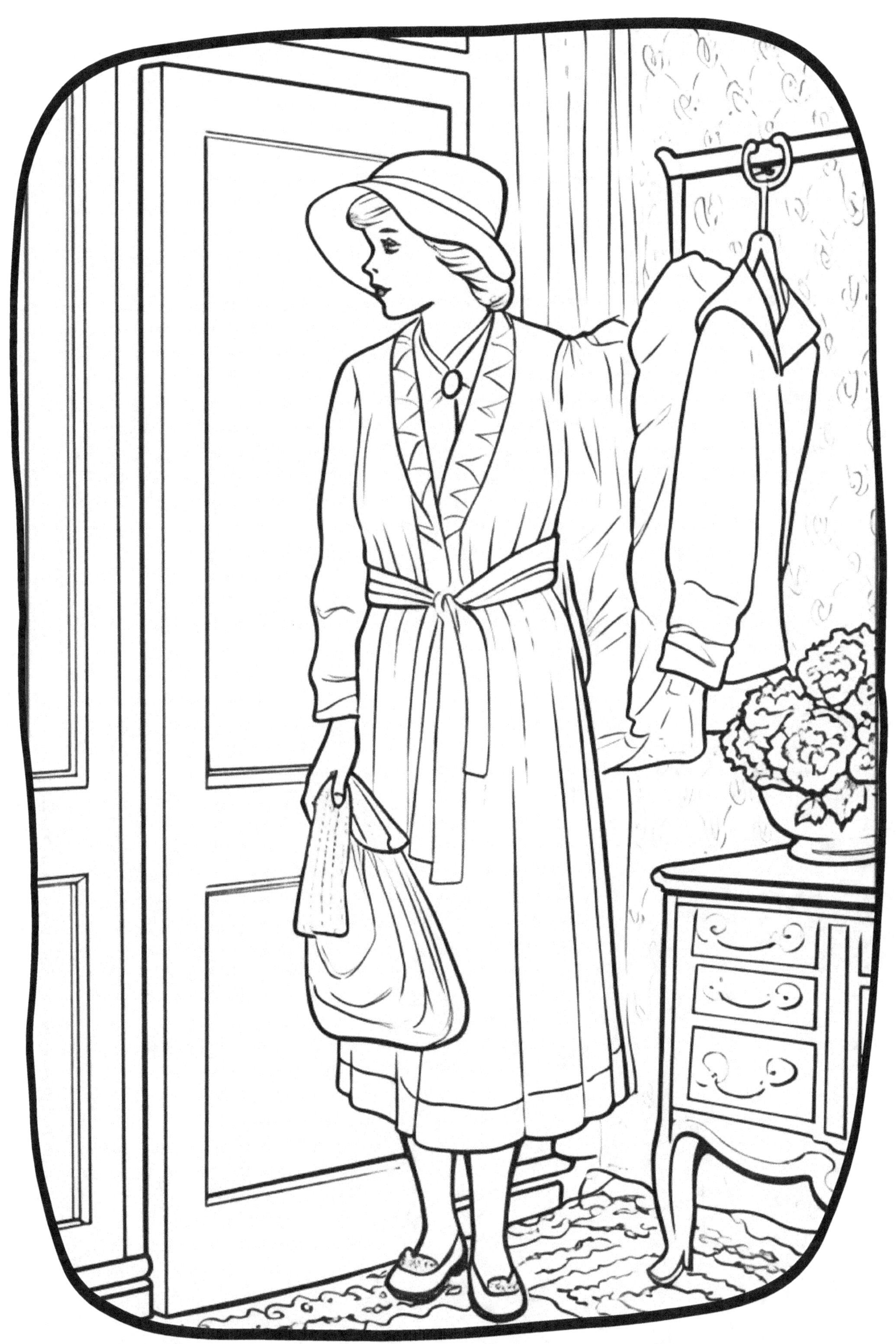

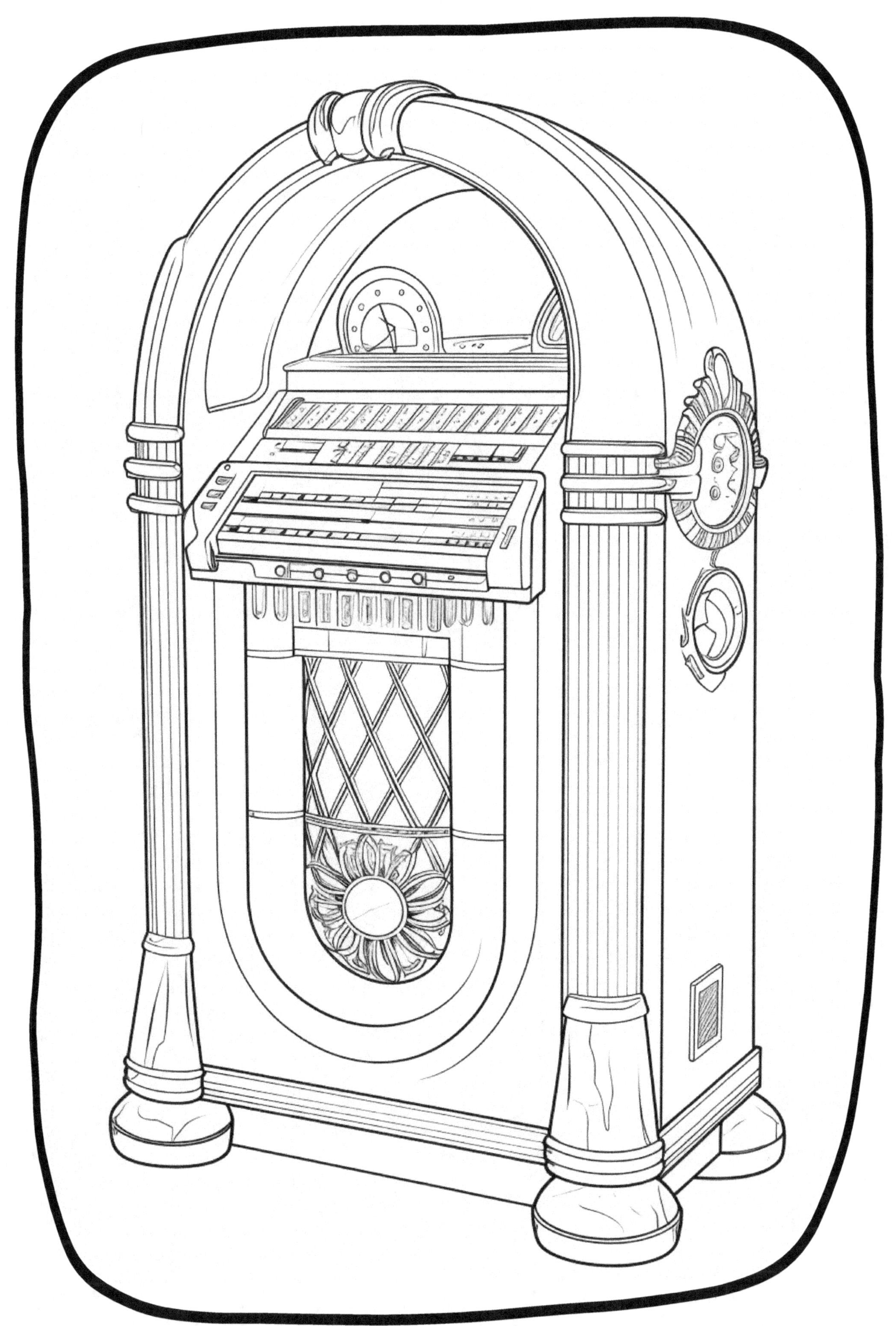

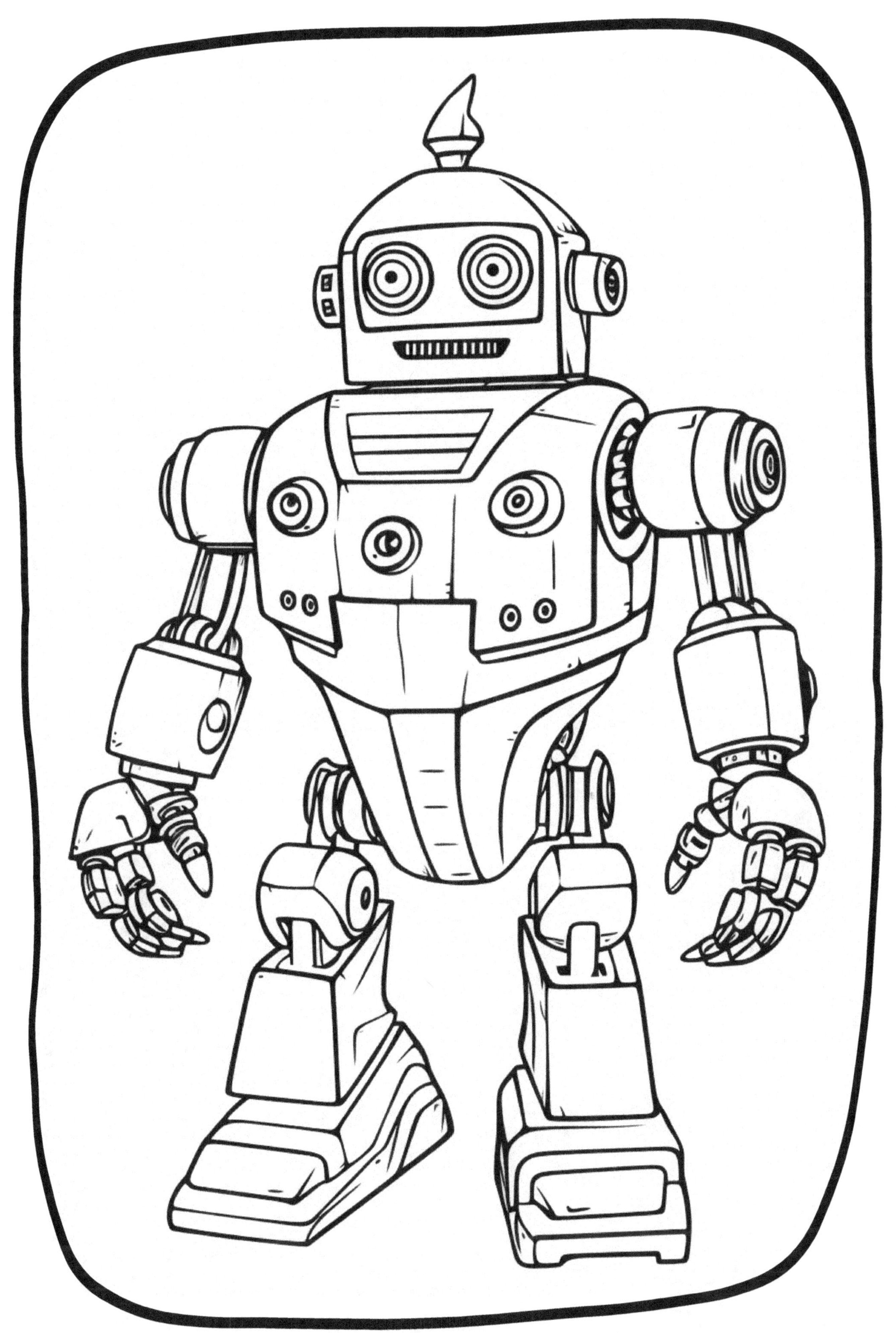

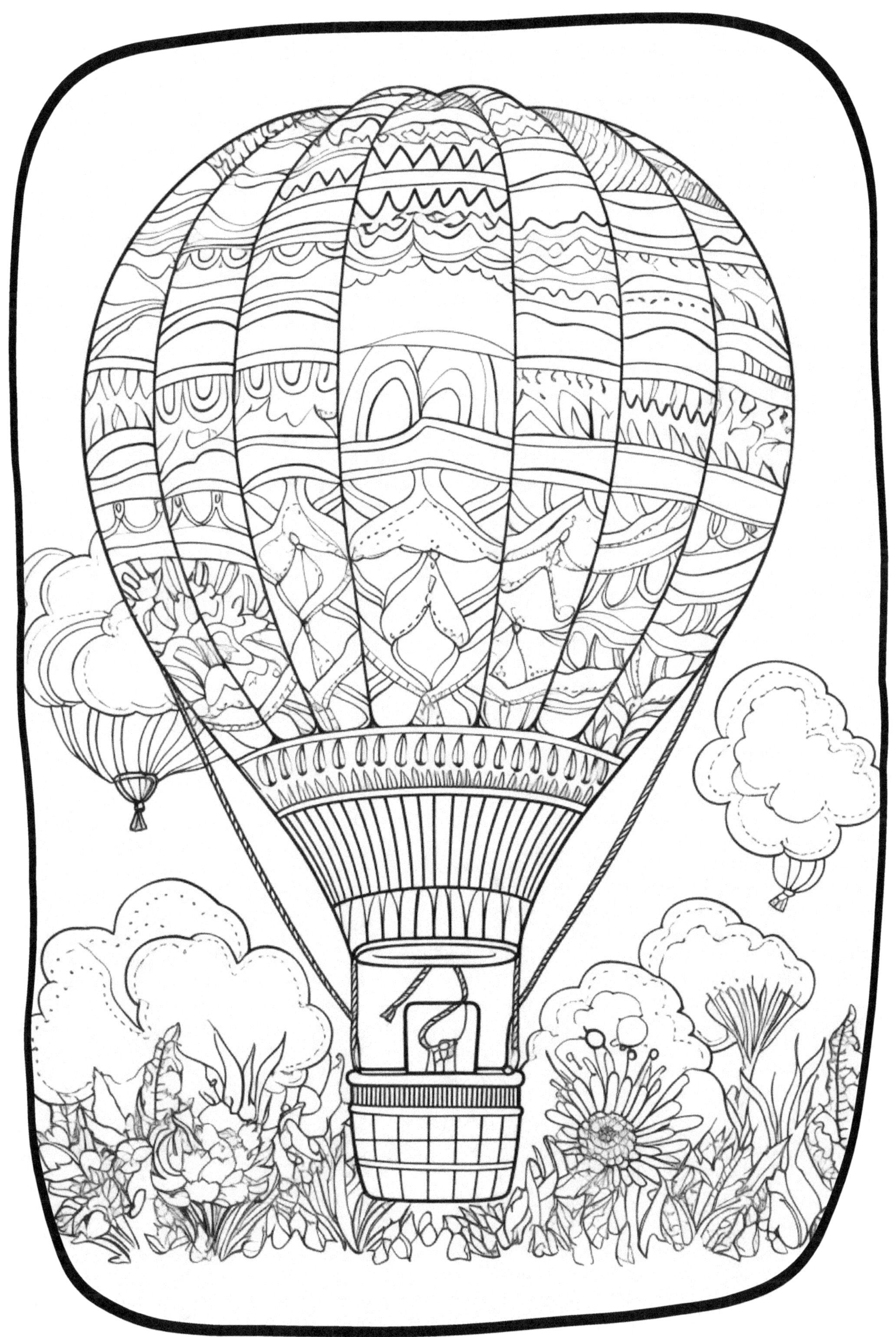

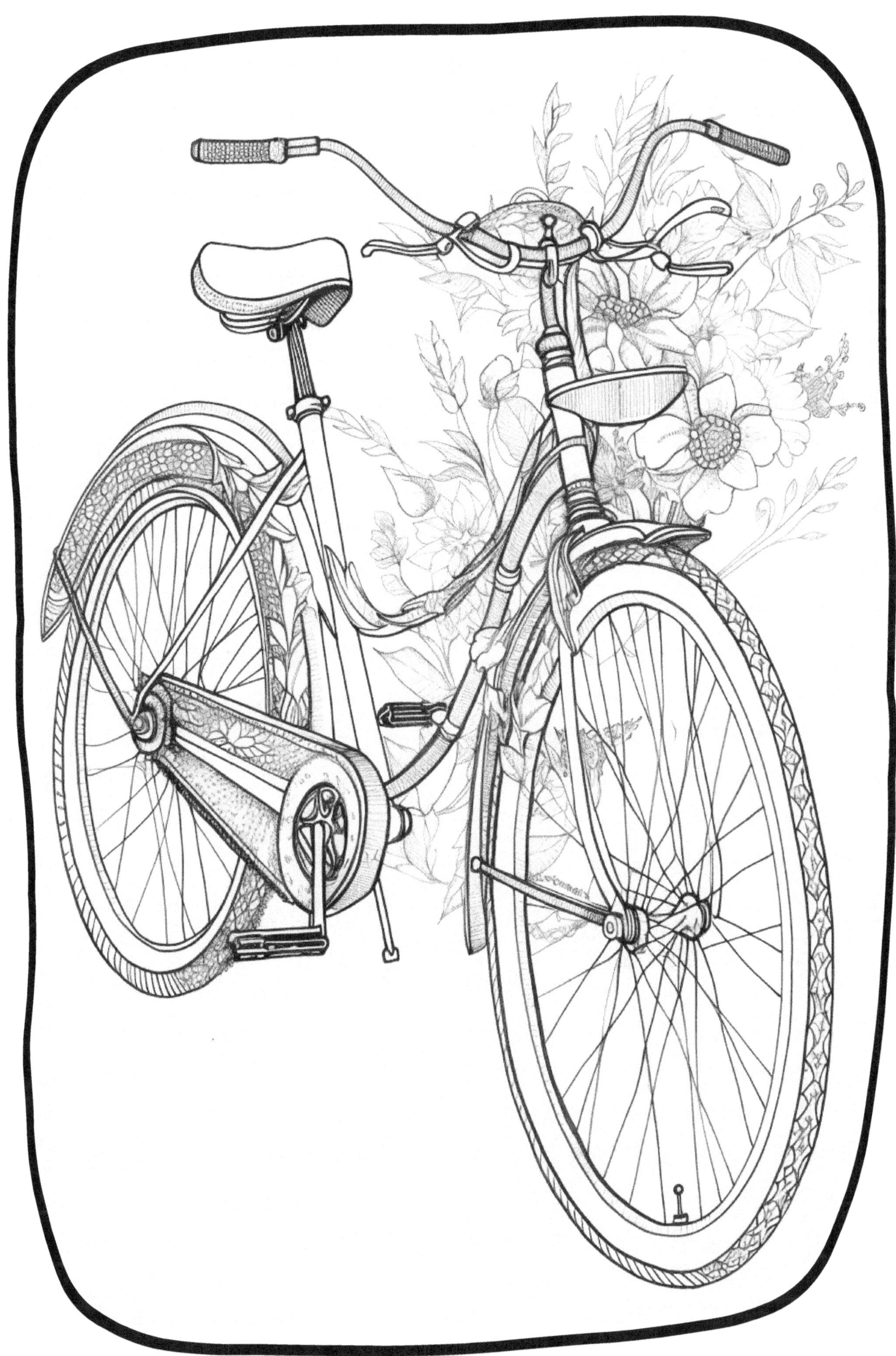

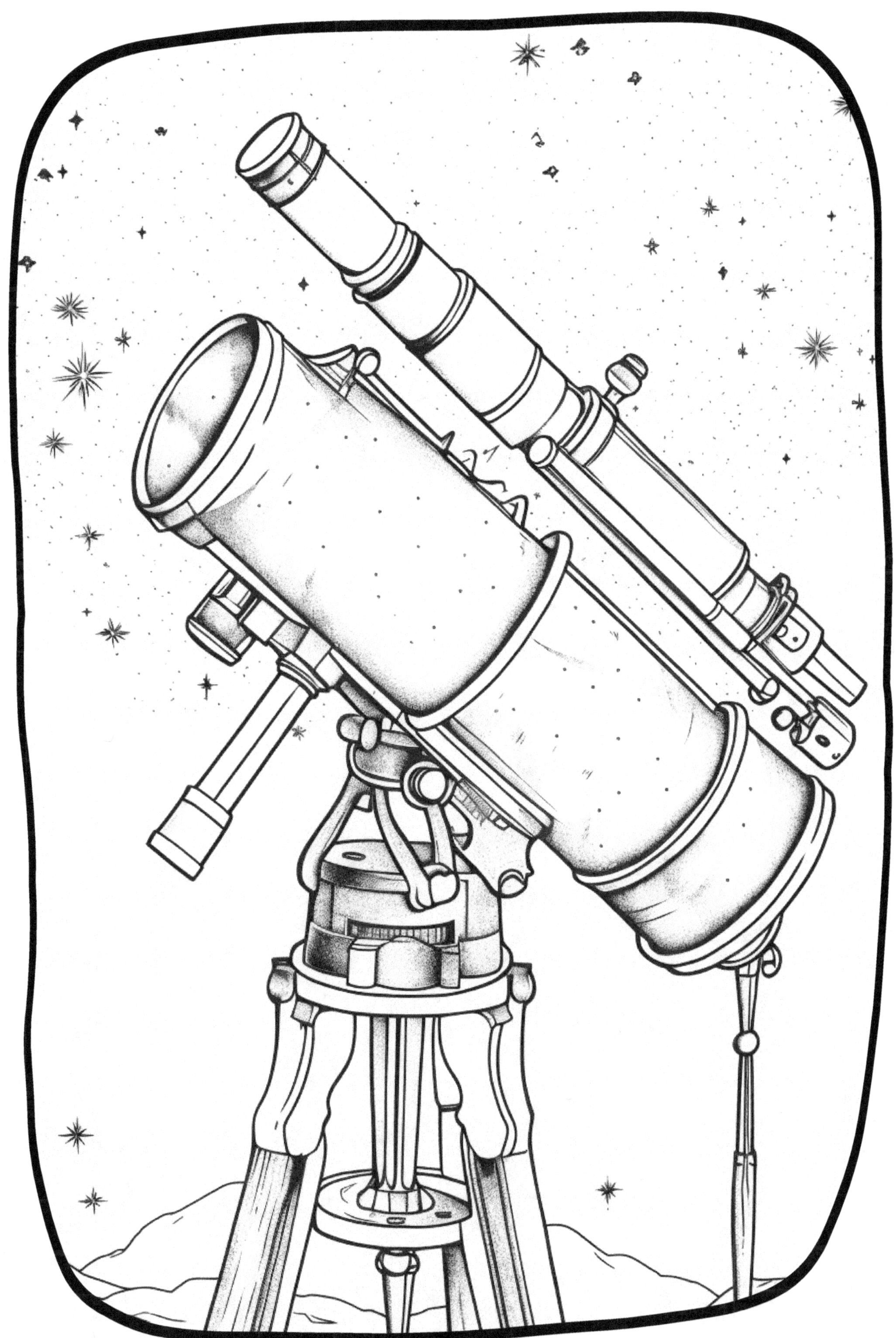

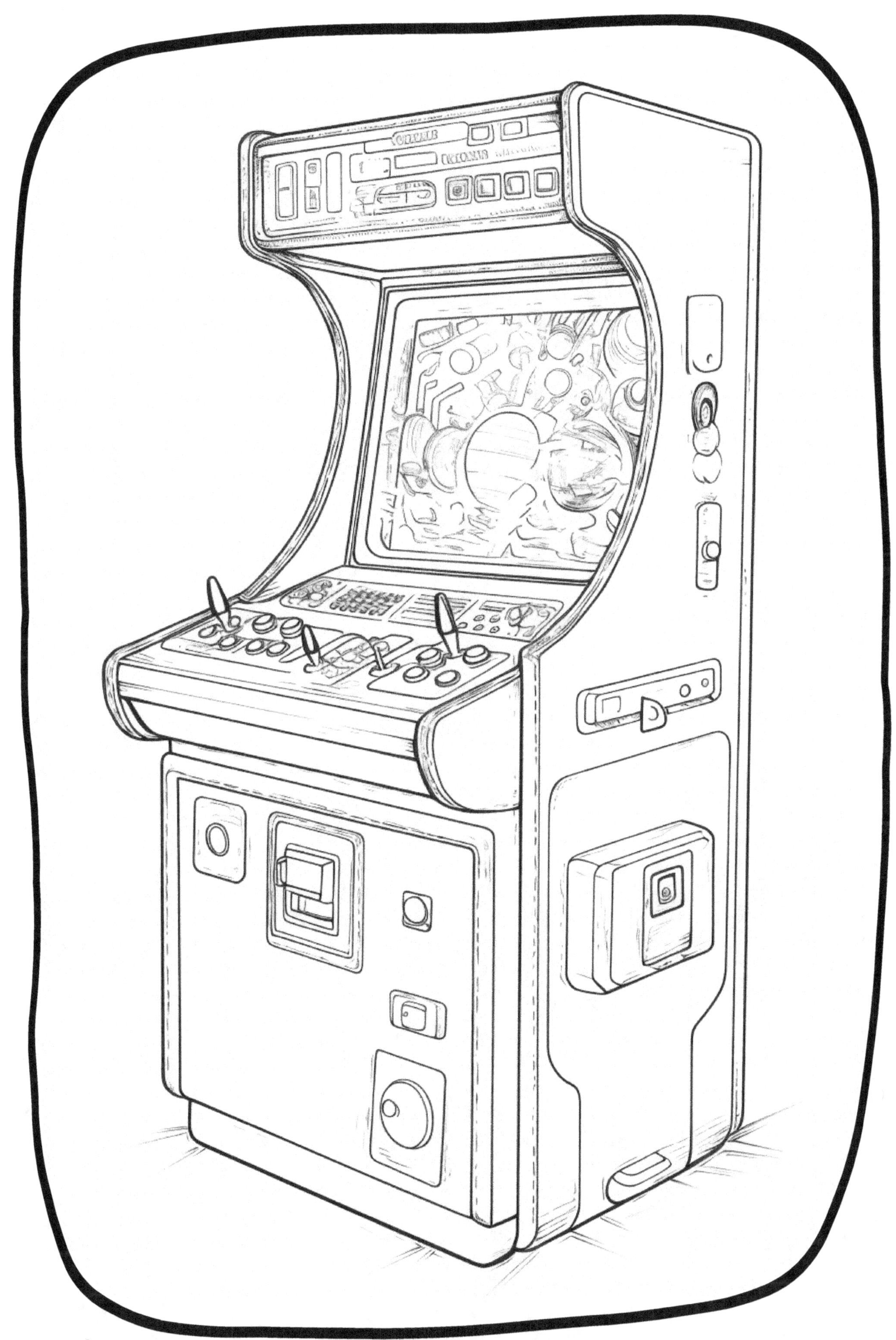

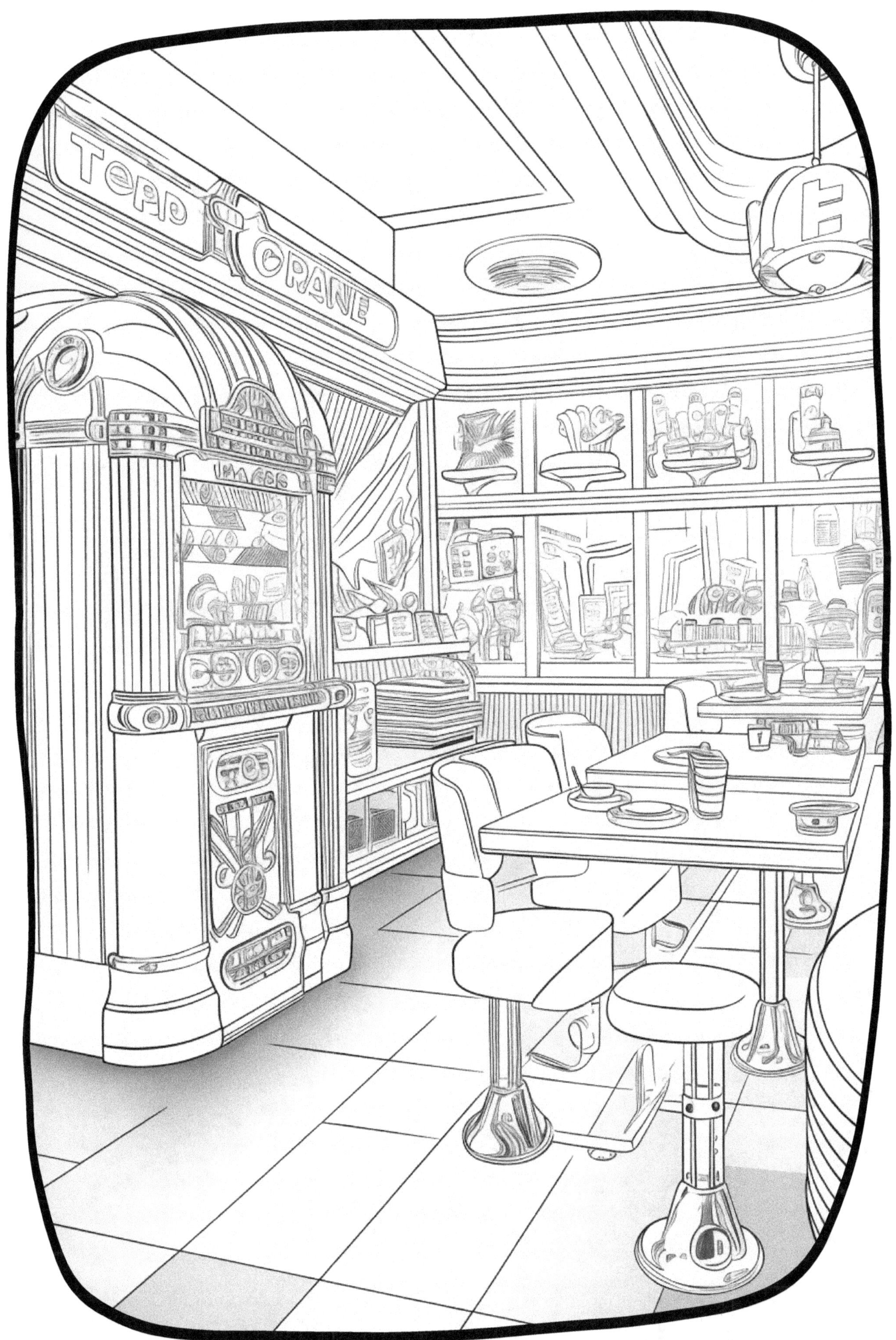
Topp
Crane

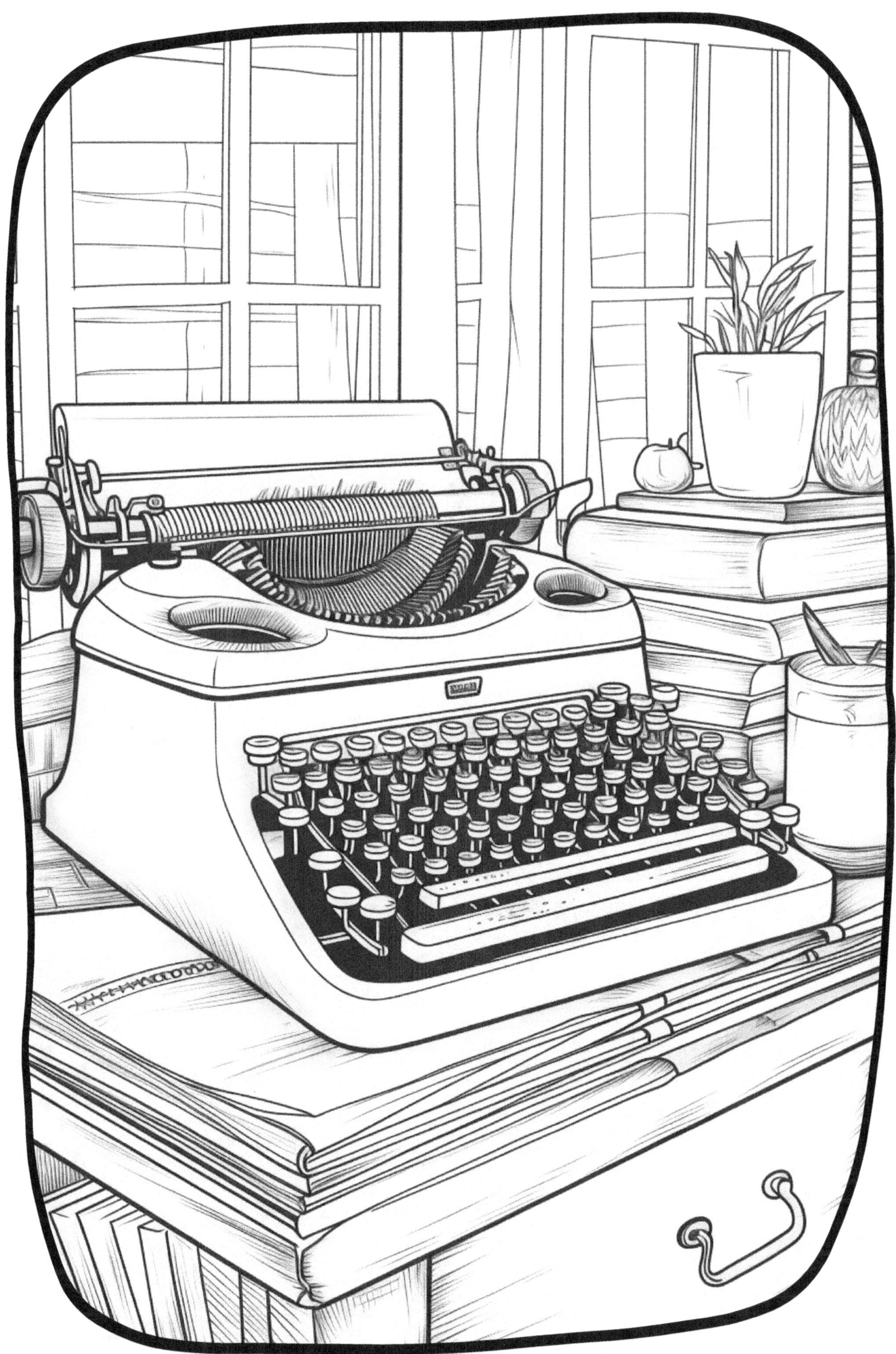

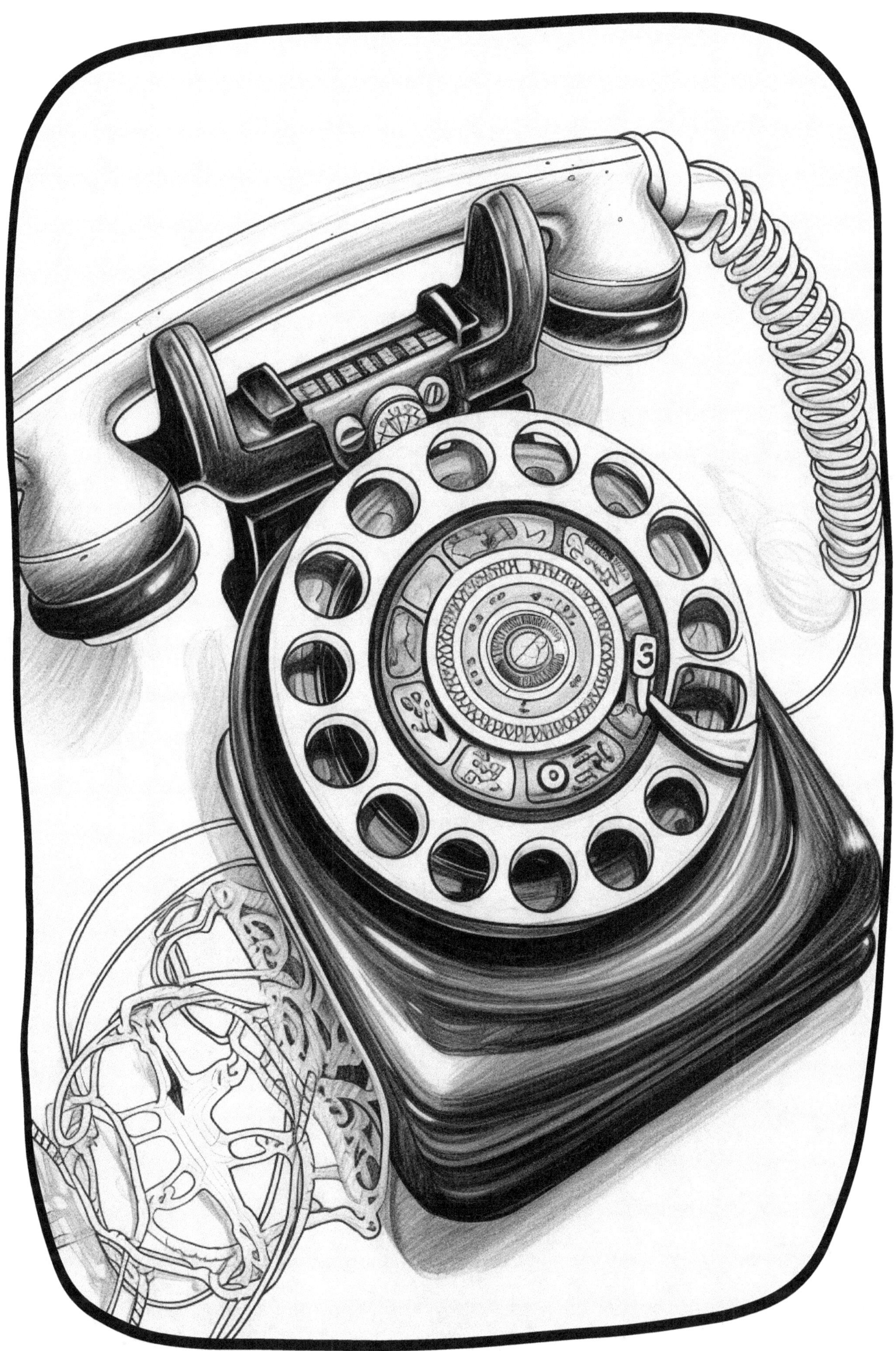

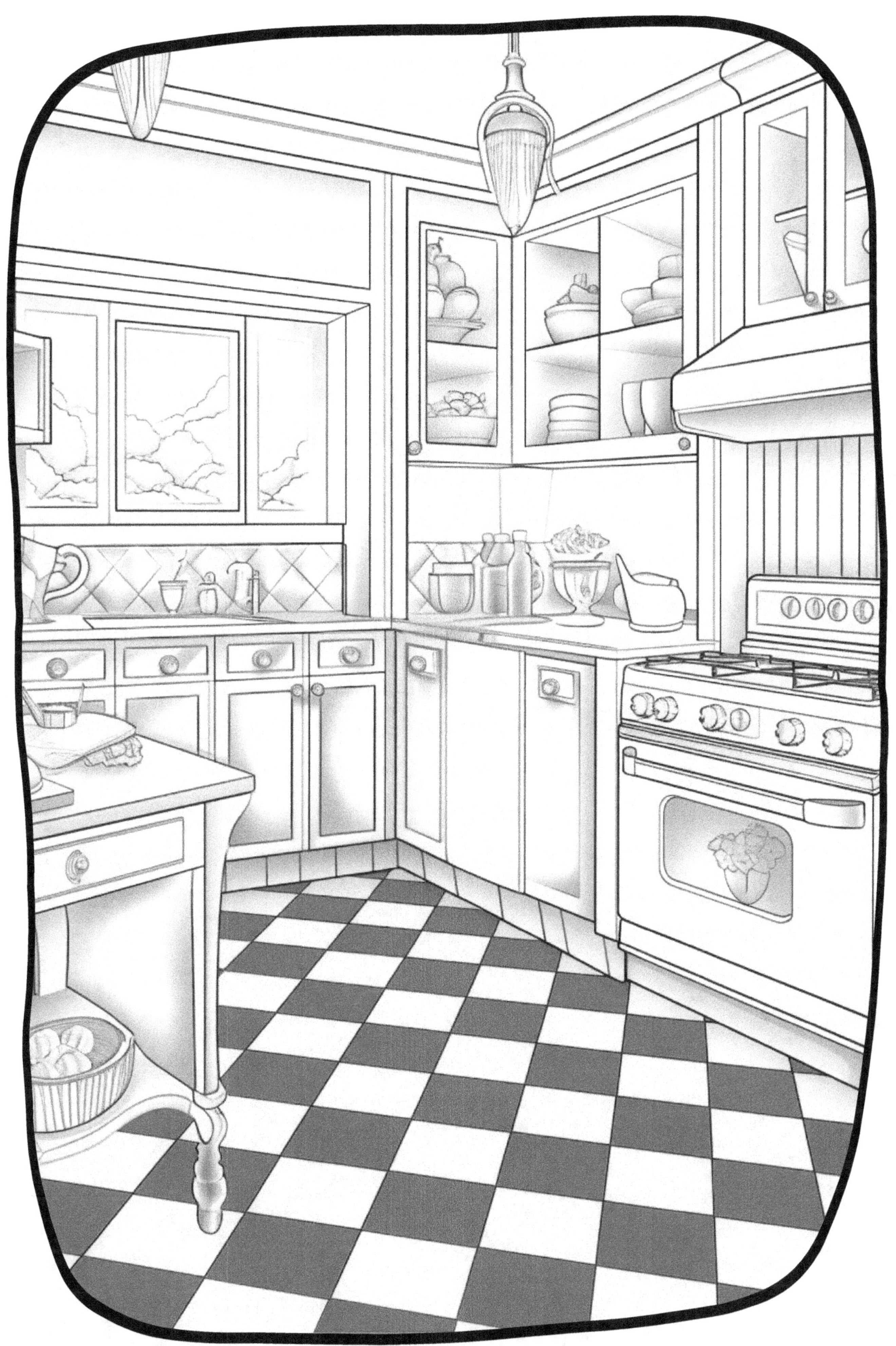

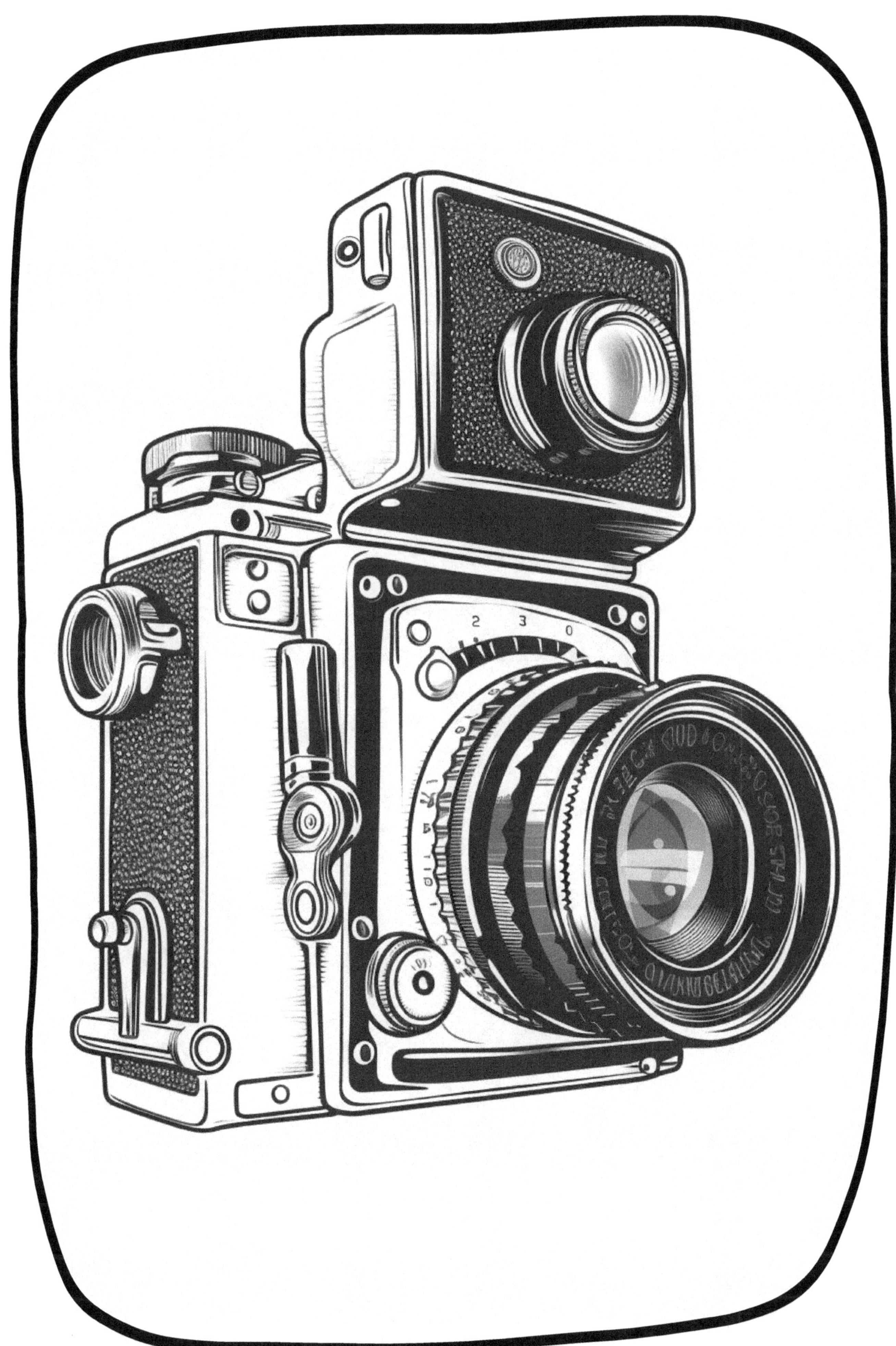

www.ingramcontent.com/pod-product-compliance
Lightning Source LLC
Chambersburg PA
CBHW081746250726
48657CB00010B/3427